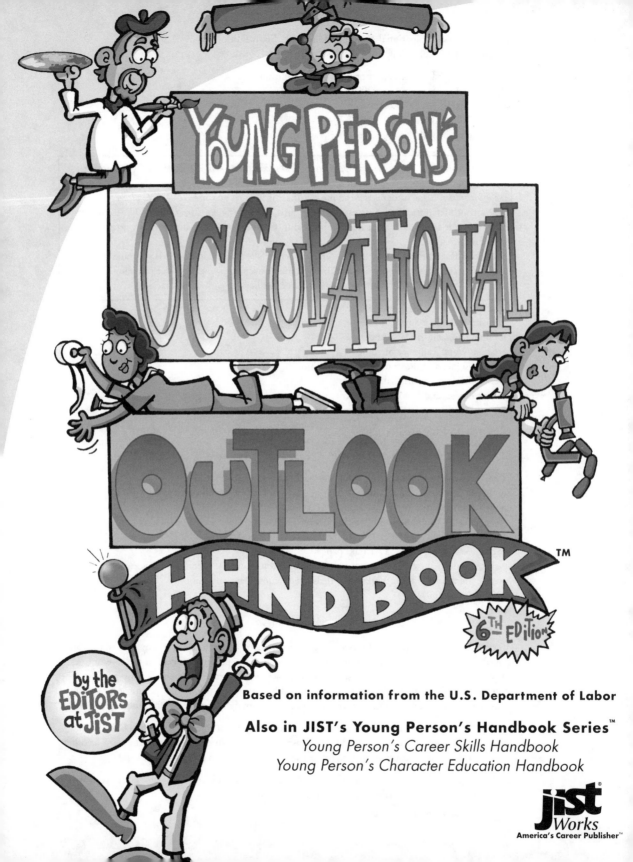

YOUNG PERSON'S OCCUPATIONAL OUTLOOK HANDBOOK™

6TH EDITION

by the EDITORS at JIST

Based on information from the U.S. Department of Labor

Also in JIST's Young Person's Handbook Series™
Young Person's Career Skills Handbook
Young Person's Character Education Handbook

JIST Works
America's Career Publisher™

Young Person's Occupational Outlook Handbook, Sixth Edition
© 2007 by JIST Publishing

Published by JIST Works, an imprint of JIST Publishing
7321 Shadeland Station, Suite 200
Indianapolis, IN 46256-3923
Phone: 800-648-JIST   Fax: 877-454-7839
E-mail: info@jist.com   Web site: www.jist.com

Note to educators. *Young Person's Occupational Outlook Handbook* is part of JIST's Young Person's Handbook Series. A corresponding workbook, *Young Person's Occupational Outlook Handbook Activities,* helps students get the most from this book. The *Career & Life Explorer* assessment matches student interests to *OOH* jobs. *Exploring Your Career Options* video inspires young people to consider their many job options. Call 800-648-JIST or visit www.jist.com for more information.

Quantity discounts are available for JIST products. Have future editions of JIST books automatically delivered to you on publication through our convenient standing order program. Please call 800-648-JIST or visit www.jist.com for a free catalog and more information.

Acquisitions Editor: Susan Pines
Development Editor: Dave Anderson
Database Work: Laurence Shatkin
Cover Designer and Illustrator: Chris Sabatino
Interior Illustrator: Chris Sabatino
Interior Design and Layout: Marie Kristine Parial-Leonardo
Proofreaders: Jeanne Clark, Paula Lowell

Printed in the United States of America

12 11 10 09 08   9 8 7 6 5 4 3 2

Library of Congress Cataloging-in-Publication Data
Young person's occupational outlook handbook / based on information from the U.S. Department of Labor ; by the editors at JIST. -- 6th ed.
     p. cm. -- (Young person's handbook series)
   Includes index.
   ISBN-13: 978-1-59357-359-1 (alk. paper)
   1. Occupations--Juvenile literature. 2. Job descriptions--Juvenile literature. 3. Vocational guidance--Juvenile literature. I. JIST Works, Inc. II. United States. Dept. of Labor.
   HF5382.Y58 2007
   331.702--dc22
                                        2006032663

We have been careful to provide accurate information throughout this book, but it is possible that errors and omissions have been introduced. Please consider this in making any career plans or other important decisions. Trust your own judgment above all else and in all things.

Trademarks: All brand names and product names used in this book are trade names, service marks, trademarks, or registered trademarks of their respective owners.

ISBN: 978-1-59357-359-1

About This Book

This book presents information on nearly 270 major jobs. These jobs cover 90 percent of the workforce, and you are very likely to work in one or more of them during your life.

In looking over these jobs, we suggest that you consider every one that interests you. Remember that you are exploring job possibilities. The information will help you learn which classes to take and what additional training or education you will need to do that job. If a job requires more training or education than you think you can get, consider it anyway. There are many ways to finance an education, so don't eliminate any job possibility too soon.

The introduction will give you useful information to help you understand and use the book for career exploration. We hope this book will help you identify some new jobs to think about and some new possibilities to consider. We wish you a happy and successful future.

CONTENTS AT A GLANCE

TABLE OF CONTENTS

Service Occupations 139

Sales & Related Occupations 167

Office & Administrative Support Occupations 181

Farming, Fishing & Forestry Occupations 217

Construction Trades & Related Workers 221

Installation, Maintenance & Repair Occupations 243

INTRODUCTION

This book is designed to help you explore a wide variety of jobs. This is important because your career choice is one of the most important decisions you will make in life. This book includes descriptions for 269 major jobs.

The job descriptions answer questions such as these:

- What do people in this job do all day?
- What training or education will I need to do the job?
- How much does the job pay?
- Will the job be in demand in the future?
- What classes should I take now to prepare me for this job?
- What jobs are related to this one?

The information in this book is based on another book called the *Occupational Outlook Handbook* (the *OOH*). The *OOH* is published by the U.S. Department of Labor and is the most widely used source of career information available. Like the *OOH*, the *Young Person's Occupational Outlook Handbook* groups similar jobs together. This makes it easy to explore related jobs you might not know about. Because the job descriptions in the *OOH* are more detailed than the ones in this book, you can refer to the *OOH* for more information on jobs that interest you.

Tips to Identify Jobs That Interest You

The table of contents lists all the jobs in this book, arranged into groups of similar jobs. Look through the list and choose one or more of the job groups that sound most interesting to you. Make a list of the jobs that interest you, and then read the descriptions for those jobs.

The Information in Each Job Description

Each job description in this book uses the same format. They all include eight sections:

On the Job: This section has a short description of the duties and working conditions for the job.

Subjects to Study: Here you'll find some high school courses that will help you prepare for the job.

Discover More: This section has an activity you can do to learn more about the job, or a place to go for more information.

Related Jobs: This section lists similar jobs you can consider.

Something Extra: This box has interesting, fun facts or stories related to the job.

Education & Training: This section tells you the education and training levels most employers expect for someone starting out in the job. Almost all jobs now require a high school diploma, so we do not include "high school graduate" as an option. Instead, we list the *additional* training or education the average high school graduate needs to get the job.

Here are the abbreviations we've used for the levels of training and education:

Short-term OJT = On-the-job training that lasts up to six months.

Moderate-term OJT = On-the-job training that lasts up to a year.

Long-term OJT = On-the-job training that lasts up to two or more years.

Work experience = Work experience in a related job.

Voc/tech training = Formal vocational or technical training received in a school, apprenticeship, or cooperative education program or in the military. This training can last from a few months to two or more years and may combine classroom training with on-the-job experience.

Associate degree = A two-year college degree.

Bachelor's degree = A four-year college degree.

Master's degree = A bachelor's degree plus one or two years of additional education.

Doctoral degree = A master's degree plus two or more years of additional education.

Professional degree = Typically, a bachelor's degree plus two or more years of specialized education (for example, education to be an attorney, physician, or veterinarian).

Plus sign (+) = The plus sign indicates that you need work experience in a related job as well as formal education. For example, "Bachelor's degree +" means that you need a bachelor's degree plus work experience in a related job.

Earnings: Dollar signs represent the approximate range of average earnings for a job.

$ = $19,000 or less per year

$$ = $19,001 to $25,000 per year

$$$ = $25,001 to $30,000 per year

$$$$ = $30,001 to $55,000 per year

$$$$$ = $55,001 or more per year

Job Outlook: This tells you whether the job is likely to employ more or fewer people in the future.

Declining = Employment is expected to decrease.

Little change = Employment is expected to remain about the same or increase as much as 8%.

Average increase = Employment is expected to increase from 9% to 17%.

Above-average increase = Employment is expected to increase from 18% to 26%.

Rapid increase = Employment is expected to increase by 27% or more.

Using the Earnings and Job Outlook Information

Are lower earnings "bad" and higher earnings "good"? Is rapid growth in a job better than slow growth or a decline?

Many people do not consider jobs if the jobs have low earnings or are not projected to grow rapidly. But we think you should look at earnings and growth as just two of several factors when you consider your job options. Here is some advice for looking at these important measures.

Earnings Information

Median earnings for an adult worker in the United States are about $29,000 a year. A four-year college graduate has median earnings about $17,000 more than that per year. There is a clear connection between earnings and education, and it goes like this: The more you learn, the more you are likely to earn. But information on earnings can be misleading. Some people earn much more than the average, even in "low-paying" jobs. For example, some waiters and waitresses earn more than $50,000 a year, although the average earnings for these jobs are much lower. Likewise, some high school graduates earn much more than the average for four-year college graduates.

Earnings also vary widely for similar jobs with different employers or in different parts of the country. Finally, young workers usually earn a lot less than the average because they have less work experience than the average worker in the same job.

This book presents earnings information for the "average" person in the job. But you should remember that half of all people in any job earn more than average, and half earn less. So don't eliminate a job that interests you based only on its average pay.

Job Outlook Information

The U.S. Department of Labor, a part of the federal government, collects job information from all over the country. The department uses some of this information to guess which jobs are likely to grow and which will decline—and by how much. The most recent information projects job growth for the next six or seven years. Some jobs will grow faster than average. Others will grow slower than average. What's more, some jobs are likely to employ fewer people in six years than they do now.

But, as with earnings, job growth should be only one of the things you consider in planning your career. For example, jobs that employ small numbers of people may have rapid growth, but they won't generate nearly as many new jobs as a slow-growing but large field like "cashier." Don't eliminate jobs that interest you simply because they are not growing quickly. Even jobs that are "declining" will have some new openings for talented people because workers leave the field for retirement or other jobs.

Some Things to Consider

Choosing your career is one of the most important decisions of your life. By exploring career options now, you will be better prepared to make good decisions later. Here are some things you should consider:

Your Interests: Think about what interests you. Your hobbies, school subjects you like or do well in, sports and clubs, home and family chores, volunteer activities, and other things can be clues to possible careers. For example, if you play an instrument or like to listen to music, you might think about a job in the music industry.

Your Values: It is important to look for a job that lets you do something you believe in. For example, if you want to help people, you will be happier in a job that allows you to do that. Or you may be able to find a hobby or volunteer job that lets you do this outside of your job. Either way, it's worth thinking about.

Education and Training: How much education or training are you willing to get? Most of the better-paying jobs today require training or education beyond high school. And more and more jobs require computer skills, technical training, or other specialized skills. It's true that more education often results in more and better job opportunities. So you might want to consider getting a four-year degree or technical training after high school. For now, you should consider any job that interests you, even if you aren't sure whether you can afford the training or education required. If you really want to do something, you can find a way.

Earnings: What you earn at your job is important because it defines what kind of lifestyle you can afford. Higher-paying jobs usually require higher levels of training or education and/or higher levels of responsibility.

Working Conditions: Would you like to work in an office or outside? Would you rather work by yourself or as part of a group? Do you want to be in charge? What kinds of people would you like to work with? These are just some of the things to consider in planning your career.

Satisfaction: You will spend hundreds of hours working each year, and you will be happier if you are doing work you enjoy and are good at. Your interests and values can give you important clues to possible jobs.

Skills: What skills do you have? What skills do you need to get the jobs you want? What skills can you learn or improve with more training or education? The skills you have already—and the skills you can develop in the future—are important parts of making good career decisions.

Self-Employment: Did you know that 8 percent of all workers are self-employed or own their own businesses today? Head to the library and you'll find lots of books and other sources of information on this topic. If self-employment appeals to you, don't let anyone tell you "you're too young." Check it out!

Getting More Information

As you can see, there are a lot of things to consider in planning your career or job options. This book can help you find the jobs that interest you. But when you're done here, you'll want to get more information. After you decide which jobs interest you, here are some places to learn more:

Check out the *Occupational Outlook Handbook:* The *OOH* has more thorough descriptions for each of the jobs in this book, so you should start there. It's available in the reference section of your library or at your local bookstore.

Visit the Library: You can find the *OOH* and many other career books, magazines, and other resources at most libraries. Ask your librarian for help in finding what you want.

Talk to People: Find people who work in jobs that interest you and "interview" them. Ask what they like and don't like about the job, how to get started, what education or training you need, and other details.

The Internet: You can find a lot of career information online. Throughout this book you will find suggested Web sites to visit. In addition, the appendix in the back of the book lists hundreds of useful Web sites as well.

Your Teacher: Ask your teacher for ideas on other sources of career information. He or she might be able to help you find more information in your school library or from other sources.

Remember, this book is only the beginning of your search for "the right career." Don't rule out any jobs because they seem out of reach or because they don't pay enough. Follow your dreams, do your homework, and you'll figure out how to get from here to there.

"All our dreams can come true—if we have the courage to pursue them."
Walt Disney

Management &
Business & Financial
Operations
Occupations

Administrative Services Managers

How comfortable is a receptionist on a cold winter day if his or her desk sits in front of an outside door? How far from a secretary's desk should the copy machines be? Should a computer printer be put outside a meeting room door? These might seem like trivial questions, but they are important factors in how a business runs. Managers in charge of business facilities design work areas that are comfortable and efficient for workers and profitable for the company.

On the Job

Administrative services managers work for large and small businesses and government agencies. They manage the services that keep businesses in business including the mailroom, food, security, parking, printing, purchasing, and payroll. In large companies, they may manage other workers. In small ones, they may be responsible for any or all of these services themselves. Facility managers plan, design, and manage workplace facilities.

Subjects to Study

English, math, speech, computer skills, economics, business courses

Education & Training
Bachelor's degree +

Earnings
$$$$$

Job Outlook
Average increase

Discover More

Divide your class into groups of four or five. Have each group take a turn planning and directing a class activity. Groups will have to decide what supplies they need for their activity, who will bring them in, and how they will teach the activity. For example, you might teach your classmates to make paper fans or create an assembly line to produce gingerbread houses.

Related Jobs

Office and administrative support worker supervisors and managers; cost estimators; property, real estate, and community association managers; purchasing managers, buyers, and purchasing agents; top executives

Advertising, Marketing, Promotions, Public Relations & Sales Managers

On the Job

These workers help businesses sell their products. Before a product ever goes on the assembly line, marketing managers decide whether it will sell and who will buy it. Advertising managers decide what type of ads will work best. Promotions and sales managers design campaigns to let the public know about the product. Public relations managers help companies create a good image in the community. All of these managers travel a lot, and job transfers are common.

SOMETHING EXTRA

Did you know that it costs nearly $2,500,000 to run a 30-second television ad during the Super Bowl? That's about $80,000 per second that companies spend trying to convince you to buy their products. Imagine spending millions of dollars on something that people might not even see because they've gone to get more chips. Now you know why advertising and marketing managers try so hard to be clever to keep your attention (and keep you from changing the channel).

Subjects to Study

English, speech, journalism, art, computer skills, business courses

Discover More

The next time you are watching TV or reading a magazine, study the commercials or ads closely. Some are funny, some serious, others just confusing. Are they effective? Do they make you want to buy the products they are promoting? How would you change an ad to make it more effective?

Education & Training
Bachelor's degree +

Earnings
$$$$$

Related Jobs

Actors, producers, and directors; advertising sales agents; artists and related workers; demonstrators, product promoters, and models; market and survey researchers; public relations specialists; sales representatives, wholesale and manufacturing; writers and editors

Job Outlook
Above-average increase

Computer & Information Systems Managers

On the Job

Computer and information systems managers plan and direct computer labs in large and small companies and for the government. They hire computer programmers and support specialists. They manage and review the work in a business and help determine salaries. They decide what workers and equipment are needed to do certain jobs, and often they are involved in the upkeep, maintenance, and security of computer networks.

Subjects to Study

Math, physics, chemistry, computer science, speech, business courses

Education & Training
Bachelor's degree +

Earnings
$$$$$

Job Outlook
Above-average increase

Discover More

Take a tour of your school's computer lab. Does the lab instructor keep the computers in running order, or does the school use an outside contractor for that job? How often are the computers updated? Are they checked regularly for viruses? These are just a few of the questions a computer systems manager must answer.

Related Jobs

Computer programmers, computer software engineers, computer systems analysts, computer scientists and database administrators, computer support specialists and systems administrators

Construction Managers

On the Job

Construction managers plan and direct construction projects. On small projects, they are responsible for all the people, materials, and equipment at a job site. They hire and schedule workers, make sure materials are delivered on time, and oversee the safety of the work site. They often work outdoors, and may be on call 24 hours a day to deal with delays, bad weather, and emergencies.

SOMETHING EXTRA

Did you ever wonder how builders choose what materials to use? Sometimes the environment decides for them. In China, for example, builders use stone and brick for construction because much of the land is treeless. In Northern California, builders cannot use wood-shingled roofs on houses because of fire hazard. In Mexico, houses are often built from mud bricks called adobe, which keeps them cool in the hot sun.

Subjects to Study

Math, shop courses, computer skills, drafting, business courses

Discover More

Taking shop courses at school, building small projects at home, and apprenticing with a skilled craft worker are some ways you can learn more about the construction industry.

Related Jobs

Architects, except landscape and naval; engineers; cost estimators; landscape architects; engineering and natural sciences managers

Education & Training
Bachelor's degree

Earnings
$$$$$

Job Outlook
Average increase

Education Administrators

On the Job

Education administrators are like the managers of schools, colleges, and universities. They develop programs, monitor students' progress, train teachers, and prepare budgets. They must communicate with parents, students, employers, and the community. They might be school principals, college presidents or deans, or school-district superintendents. Many education administrators begin their careers as teachers.

Subjects to Study

English, speech, computer skills, statistics, psychology

Education & Training
Bachelor's degree +

Earnings
$$$$$

Job Outlook
Average increase

Discover More

Ask the principal or dean at your school if you can "apprentice" with him or her for a day, watching, asking questions, and helping out as needed. Does the workday end when school is out? Will you have to attend evening meetings? Are there aspects of the job you like or dislike?

Related Jobs

Administrative services managers; office and administrative support worker supervisors and managers; human resources, training, and labor relations managers and specialists; counselors; librarians; instructional coordinators; teachers—preschool, kindergarten, elementary, middle, and secondary; teachers—postsecondary

Engineering & Natural Sciences Managers

On the Job

Engineering and natural science managers plan and direct research, development, and production in large and small companies and research labs. They hire engineers, chemists, and biologists. They manage and review the work in a business or lab and help determine salaries. They also decide what workers and equipment are needed to do certain jobs. Most of them begin their careers as engineers or scientists and work their way up to managerial positions.

SOMETHING EXTRA

Twenty years ago, the title engineering manager almost always brought up the image of a man in a lab coat. But in the last two decades, the field has opened to women. In fact, today's engineering companies are actively recruiting women at all levels of employment. Current statistics show the results: Nearly 25 percent of all engineering and science managers today are women, although that's still below the average of 45 percent for all occupations.

Subjects to Study

Math, physics, chemistry, shop courses, computer skills, English, speech, business courses

Discover More

Ask to shadow your own school lab coordinator for a day or two. What kinds of jobs does he or she perform on a regular basis? This might include supervising other workers and volunteers, keeping track of chemicals and other supplies, and preparing workstations.

Related Jobs

Engineers, mathematicians, agricultural and food scientists, atmospheric scientists, biological scientists, conservation scientists and foresters, chemists and materials scientists, environmental scientists and hydrologists, geoscientists, medical scientists, top executives

Education & Training
Bachelor's degree +

Earnings
$$$$$

Job Outlook
Average increase

Farmers, Ranchers & Agricultural Managers

Say the word farmer, and most of us picture a man in overalls riding a tractor or perhaps milking a cow. Some farmers do those things, of course, but others hardly fit this image. Fish farmers in Georgia tend large lakes of small fish. Citrus farmers in Florida spend cold evenings covering tender trees with plastic to keep their fruits from freezing. Grape growers in the Napa Valley test their grapes for just the right sweetness before selling them to wine makers. There are as many kinds of farmers as there are products to eat!

On the Job

Because of the chemicals and equipment used, farming and ranching are dangerous jobs. Farmers on crop farms work dawn to dusk through the growing season to produce the grains, fruits, and vegetables that feed the country. During the rest of the year, many work second jobs. On ranches, animals must be fed and watered every day and fences must be inspected regularly. Aquaculture farmers are responsible for raising fish. Farmers and ranchers must also have good business skills, as many of the farms in the United States are still family owned and operated.

Subjects to Study

Life sciences, shop courses, math, business, computer skills

Discover More

Planting, tending, and harvesting your own vegetable or flower garden is a good way to learn about crop farming. To learn more about animal farming, you could raise a small animal through the 4-H program in your community.

Related Jobs

Agricultural and food scientists; agricultural workers; purchasing managers, buyers, and purchasing agents

Education & Training
Long-term OJT to Bachelor's degree +

Earnings
$$$$

Job Outlook
Declining

Financial Managers

On the Job

Financial managers work for all kinds of businesses. Many work for banks, credit unions, or insurance companies. They prepare financial reports and make sure the business pays its taxes and has enough money to operate. They watch over the cash flow, manage the company's stocks, and communicate with investors. They also decide whether the business needs to borrow money, lend money, or invest in stocks and bonds.

SOMETHING EXTRA

Managing a company's finances is a huge responsibility. Not only do the company and its employees rely on you to manage the money, but the investors do as well. Sometimes the power given to financial officers gets abused, as was the case with Enron, an energy company based in Texas. Their fraudulent activity resulted in the bankruptcy of the company and the loss of thousands of employees' and investors' savings, proving that with great power comes great responsibility.

Subjects to Study

Math, English, business courses, accounting, writing, computer skills, speech, foreign languages

Discover More

Learn more about investing in the stock market by checking out these sites on the Internet:

The Young Investor: www.younginvestor.com

Kids' Money: www.kidsmoney.org

EduStock: http://library.thinkquest.org/3088/

Related Jobs

Accountants and auditors; budget analysts; financial analysts and personal financial advisors; insurance sales agents; insurance underwriters; loan officers; securities, commodities, and financial services sales agents; real estate brokers and sales agents

Education & Training
Bachelor's degree +

Earnings
$$$$$

Job Outlook
Average increase

Food Service Managers

Have you ever heard of Hamburger University? Students come from around the world to attend McDonald's manager training school in Oak Brook, Illinois. There, they learn about maintaining product quality, hiring and supervising workers, advertising and publicity, equipment repair, and other aspects of restaurant management. The training lasts two weeks, and graduates are qualified to manage a McDonald's restaurant.

On the Job

Food service managers select and price the food on a restaurant's menu. They hire and train workers and manage staffing, payroll, and bookkeeping. They also oversee the preparation of food, order supplies and ingredients, and make sure the restaurant is clean and well maintained. Many managers work nights and weekends, often under stressful circumstances.

Subjects to Study

Math, English, business courses, nutrition, family and consumer sciences, psychology, accounting

Discover More

The best way to learn about the food industry is to work in it. Consider taking a summer job at a local restaurant waiting tables, busing tables, or washing dishes. If you prefer not to get your hands dirty, you can at least talk to someone who works in a restaurant about what they like best about the job.

Related Jobs

Lodging managers, sales worker supervisors, food and beverage serving and related workers

Education & Training
Work experience

Earnings
$$$$

Job Outlook
Average increase

Funeral Directors

On the Job

Funeral directors, also called morticians or undertakers, prepare bodies for burial or cremation. When someone dies, they help the family plan the funeral, prepare the obituary notice, and handle the paperwork. Most are licensed embalmers. Funeral directors are also businesspeople: They pre-pare bills, keep financial records, and hire and manage a staff. Most work long, irregular hours.

SOMETHING EXTRA

More and more people are opting for cremation these days. And people sometimes choose unusual ways to deal with their ashes. "Star Trek" creator Gene Rod-denberry's ashes were carried into space on the space shuttle; 1960s rock icon Janis Joplin's were scattered off the California coast; and John Lennon's were wrapped as a Christmas gift and delivered to his wife, Yoko Ono. Perhaps the strangest of all was author Hunter S. Thompson, who had his ashes blasted out of a cannon!

Subjects to Study

Business courses, English, biology, chemistry, psychology

Discover More

Take a class trip to a local funeral home. Ask the direc-tor about his or her job: Does the director do much counseling with grieving families? Does he or she also do embalming—preparing bodies for burial? Does the funeral home offer cremation services as well? Has the director had clients who have made unusual requests for their ashes?

Related Jobs

Social workers, psychologists, physicians and surgeons

Education & Training
Associate degree

Earnings
$$$$

Job Outlook
Little change

Human Resources, Training & Labor Relations Managers & Specialists

On the Job

These workers find the best employees they can and match those new employees with jobs in their company. They inter-view job candidates and train new workers. They may travel to college campuses to find the best job applicants. They help to resolve con-flicts among workers or between workers and management. They also provide some employee training and are concerned with maintaining worker satisfaction.

Subjects to Study

English, business courses, psychology, sociology, communication skills, writ-ing, computer skills, foreign languages

Education & Training

Bachelor's degree to Bachelor's degree +

Earnings

$$$$$

Job Outlook

Above-average increase

Discover More

If your school has a conflict-resolution team, volunteer to participate. If it does not, set up a team in your class-room. The team's job is to help out when two students are involved in a dispute. Team members hear both sides and come up with a fair solution. They might also teach conflict-resolution skills to other students.

Related Jobs

Counselors, education administrators, public relations specialists, lawyers, psychologists, social and human ser-vice assistants, social workers

Industrial Production Managers

On the Job

These workers direct scheduling, staffing, equipment, quality control, and inventory in factories. Their main job is to get goods produced on time and within budget. They decide what equipment and workers to use and in what order. They also monitor the production run to make sure it stays on schedule and to fix any problems that arise.

SOMETHING EXTRA

You have to have 10,000 widgets ready by Wednesday. Your widget painter cannot run at the same time as your widget packer. Your widget tops are arriving tomorrow, but the bottoms won't be in until the next day. On top of that, your widget-assembling workers charge double time if they have to work nights (and don't even think about asking widget workers to work on weekends). You must decide the best way to run the assembly line, when to run each machine, and whether to have your workers work overtime. And you must decide it all by noon. You're a production manager!

Subjects to Study

Math, English, shop courses, computer skills, business courses

Discover More

Plan an assembly-line process for making a craft. How many workers do you need? What materials and equipment will you use? How long will it take to make the item? How much will it cost? These are the questions a manager must answer.

Related Jobs

Engineers, management analysts, operations research analysts

Education & Training
Work experience

Earnings
$$$$$

Job Outlook
Little change

Lodging Managers

On the Job

Lodging managers hire, train, and supervise the people who work in hotels, motels, and bed-and-breakfast inns. They set room rates, handle billing, order food and supplies, and oversee the day-to-day operations. Managers who work for hotel chains may organize and staff a new hotel, refurbish an older one, or reorganize one that is not operating well. Most work more than 40 hours a week, often at night and on weekends.

Subjects to Study

English, foreign languages, business courses, math, accounting, computer skills

Discover More

Call a local hotel and ask if you can "shadow" the front desk manager for a day. Ask about job responsibilities. What kinds of hours are required? How does the manager handle unpleasant customers? What emergencies has he or she faced in the last year?

Related Jobs

Food service managers; sales worker supervisors; property, real estate, and community association managers

Education & Training
Work experience

Earnings
$ $ $ $

Job Outlook
Average increase

Medical & Health Services Managers

On the Job

Medical and health services managers—also called health care administrators—plan, organize, and supervise the delivery of health care. They determine staffing and equipment needs and direct the public relations, marketing, and finances of hospitals, nursing homes, clinics, and doctor's offices. They may be in charge of an entire organization or only one department within it. These managers earn high salaries, but they often work long hours.

SOMETHING EXTRA

Imagine it's 10 degrees below zero outside, and half of the staff members of your nursing home can't make it to work. Most of the elderly residents have the flu. The doctor on call is stuck in the snow somewhere. Whose responsibility is it to make sure the residents are safe, fed, and well cared for? If you're the manager, it's your job!

Subjects to Study

Math, English, speech, writing skills, business courses, psychology, health

Discover More

To learn more about careers in the health-care field, try volunteering at a local nursing home or hospital in your community. Many have volunteers who read to or visit with patients and make small deliveries.

Related Jobs

Insurance underwriters

Education & Training
Bachelor's degree +

Earnings
$$$$$

Job Outlook
Above-average increase

Property, Real Estate & Community Association Managers

On the Job

Property and real estate managers oversee apartment buildings, rental houses, businesses, and shopping malls. They sell empty space to renters, prepare leases, collect rent, and handle the bookkeeping. They also make sure the property is maintained and handle complaints from renters. Community association managers work for condominium or neighborhood owners' associations. Many of these managers spend much of their time away from the office.

Subjects to Study

Math, English, foreign languages, computer skills, business courses, accounting, shop courses

Education & Training
Bachelor's degree

Earnings
$$$$

Job Outlook
Average increase

Discover More

Visit an apartment complex in your community and spend a day with the manager. Ask about the best and worst parts of the job, problems he or she sees in a typical week, and what kind of training you need for this job.

Related Jobs

Administrative services managers, education administrators, food service managers, lodging managers, medical and health services managers, real estate brokers and sales agents, urban and regional planners

Purchasing Managers, Buyers & Purchasing Agents

On the Job

These workers look for the best merchandise at the lowest price for their employers or for resale. They find the best products, negotiate the price, and make sure the right amount is received at the right time. They study sales records and inventory levels, identify suppliers, and stay aware of changes in the marketplace. Many spend several days a month traveling.

SOMETHING EXTRA

Were you born to shop? Do you love the mall? Are you a trendsetter? Buyers for department stores travel the world, attending fashion shows, visiting garment factories, and checking out small boutiques. They haggle for the best possible prices. And when their work is done, they can stroll through the malls and see their choices on clothes racks, in store windows, and on other shoppers!

Subjects to Study

Math, business courses, economics, English, speech, computer skills

Discover More

Think of your family as a business. Help your parents compile a weekly "supplies" list. Then do some comparison-shopping. Call or visit several stores to see who offers the best prices on the things your family needs. Will you save money if you buy in bulk? Should you buy from more than one source? How much can you save using coupons? See how much money you can save your family "business" in one week.

Education & Training
Work experience to Bachelor's degree +

Earnings
$$$$

Related Jobs

Advertising, marketing, promotions, public relations, and sales managers; food service managers; insurance sales agents; lodging managers; sales engineers; sales representatives, wholesale and manufacturing

Job Outlook
Little change

Top Executives

On the Job

Top executives make policies and direct operations at businesses and government agencies. They decide a company's goals and make plans to meet them. They meet with other executives, boards of directors, government heads, and consultants to talk about things that could affect their business. They are responsible for the business's ultimate success or failure, and so are always under pressure.

Subjects to Study

English, business courses, accounting, speech, computer skills, psychology, math

Discover More

You can learn more about being a leader by running for the student council at your school, taking a leadership position in a club or organization, or helping to plan activities at your school, church, or home.

Related Jobs

Administrative services managers; education administrators; financial managers; food service managers; advertising, marketing, promotions, public relations, and sales managers

Education & Training
Bachelor's degree +

Earnings
$$$$$

Job Outlook
Average increase

Accountants & Auditors

On the Job

Accountants and auditors prepare and check financial reports and taxes. They work for businesses and banks, the government, and individuals. Some are self-employed, working as consultants or preparing people's tax returns. Most use computers in their work.

SOMETHING EXTRA

In the 1920s, a big-talking gangster named Al Capone boasted that he owned the city of Chicago, and he was nearly right. The police seemed helpless to bring him down—until government accountants saved the day. Capone was finally convicted and imprisoned, not for the murders he ordered or the illegal drug-running he planned, but for the taxes he didn't pay.

Subjects to Study

Math, speech, business courses, economics, computer skills, accounting

Discover More

With your teacher's help, set up a banking system in your classroom. You can earn "class dollars" for good behavior, turning in work on time, and good attendance. You can spend those dollars on items from the "class store" or maybe on special privileges. Keep your bankbook up to date, recording each dollar you earn and each one you spend at the class store. At the end of each week, help your teacher perform an "audit" of the class's earning and spending.

Education & Training
Bachelor's degree

Related Jobs

Budget analysts; cost estimators; loan officers; financial analysts and personal financial advisors; tax examiners, collectors, and revenue agents; bill and account collectors; bookkeeping, accounting, and auditing clerks; computer programmers; computer software engineers; computer support specialists and systems administrators

Earnings
$$$$$

Job Outlook
Above-average increase

Appraisers & Assessors of Real Estate

On the Job

Real estate appraisers and assessors estimate the value of all kinds of property, from farmland to shopping centers. Their evaluations are used to help decide property taxes, mortgages, or whether property is a good investment for a client. They spend much of their time researching and writing reports, but they also get out of the office frequently to do on-site evaluations.

Subjects to Study

English, math, business courses, economics, geography, computer skills

Discover More

Do your own appraisal of your house or apartment building. Write down all of the features you see (such as a garage, fireplace, or patio) and note the condition of both the land and the building. Is the roof in good shape? Does the lawn need work? Write up a report of everything you see that could be improved and show it to a parent or guardian.

Education & Training
Voc/tech training

Earnings
$$$$

Job Outlook
Above-average increase

Related Jobs

Construction and building inspectors; real estate brokers and sales agents; urban and regional planners; claims adjusters, appraisers, examiners and investigators; cost estimators

Budget Analysts

On the Job

Budget analysts help businesses decide how much money they need in order to run and how best to spend that money. They check reports and accounts during the year to make sure the business is staying within its budget and spending its money wisely. They also look for ways companies can save money and use it more efficiently.

SOMETHING EXTRA

Several years ago, newspapers across the country ran stories about the government buying $700 toilet seats. What was going on? The Defense Department had been buying items from the same companies for years, without checking to see whether it was getting a fair price. Budget analysts were called in to clear up the mess, ensuring that your tax dollars won't be spent on overpriced toilet seats again. Hopefully they stopped buying $400 hammers as well.

Subjects to Study

Math, business courses, economics, computer skills, statistics, accounting

Discover More

Imagine you are starting a business making widgets. Give yourself $10,000 to start, and then decide how to spend the money. Do you need employees? How much will you pay them? What equipment and supplies do you need? Do you have to rent work space? Make a budget for your business. Can you make a profit?

Related Jobs

Accountants and auditors, cost estimators, economists, financial analysts and personal financial advisors, financial managers, loan officers, management analysts

Education & Training
Bachelor's degree

Earnings
$$$$$

Job Outlook
Average increase

Claims Adjusters, Appraisers, Examiners & Investigators

On the Job

Insurance claims adjusters and claims investigators check to make sure that claims filed are covered by their company's policies. Then they decide how much should be paid and okay the payment. If the claim is not covered, they deny payment.

Appraisers travel to see damaged property and assess how much the damage is worth. Sometimes investigators check out suspicious or unusual claims for fraud.

Subjects to Study

Math, English, computer skills, economics, business courses, accounting, foreign languages, psychology, health

Discover More

Ask your parents if they have ever filed a claim on their car, home, life, or health insurance. Find out what they did to file the claim. Did they talk to an adjuster? Was the claim paid? Did their insurance rate go up?

Related Jobs

Cost estimators; bill and account collectors; medical records and health information technicians; billing and posting clerks and machine operators; credit authorizers, checkers, and clerks; bookkeeping, accounting, and auditing clerks; construction and building inspectors; accountants and auditors; private detectives and investigators; automotive body and related repairers

Education & Training
Long-term OJT

Earnings
$$$$

Job Outlook
Average increase

Cost Estimators

On the Job

When a company is thinking about developing a new product, the owner needs to know how much it will cost to produce. What new machinery will be needed? How much will materials cost? How many workers will be hired? A cost estimator finds the least-expensive way to make the best product. Cost estimators decide what supplies to use, find the best prices, estimate labor costs, and report back to the owner.

SOMETHING EXTRA

A company called a cost estimator to estimate the value of a load of scrap copper in the Mojave Desert. The manager warned the estimator that he might have trouble with the job. When the estimator arrived on site, he understood why. The company had been having such problems with thieves, it had dug a huge pit and put the copper inside. Then, for security, it had thrown in a bunch of rattlesnakes on top of the copper. The estimator peered into the pit, made his best guess, and high-tailed it home!

Subjects to Study

Math, computer skills, business courses, English, economics, statistics

Discover More

Plan a business making birdhouses from craft sticks. Decide how many you will make, then find the total cost of producing them. Include all your building materials (craft sticks, glue, and paint, for example), supplies (how about a hot-glue gun?), and labor costs (what you pay your helpers). How much must you charge for your birdhouses to make a profit?

Education & Training
Work experience

Earnings
$$$$

Related Jobs

Accountants and auditors, budget analysts, economists, financial analysts and personal financial advisors, insurance underwriters, loan officers, market and survey researchers, operations research analysts

Job Outlook
Above-average increase

Financial Analysts & Personal Financial Advisors

On the Job

Financial analysts help businesses decide how to invest their money safely and wisely. Many are employed full-time by the companies they advise; others work as consultants, helping many different companies. Personal financial advisors provide the same kinds of services to individuals. Many personal advisors are self-employed. These workers often put in more than 40 hours a week and may teach classes and seminars as well.

Subjects to Study

Math, English, business courses, accounting, computer skills, economics, foreign languages

Education & Training
Bachelor's degree

Earnings
$$$$$

Job Outlook
Above-average increase

Discover More

A good way to learn about investing is to do it yourself. Look through the financial pages of your newspaper or the *Wall Street Journal*. Pick two or three stocks—ones that look like safe investments or ones that seem to be growing. Pretend that you've invested $1,000 in each, then track them for a month. Will you make money or lose it?

Related Jobs

Accountants and auditors; financial managers; insurance sales agents; real estate brokers and sales agents; securities, commodities, and financial services sales representatives

Insurance Underwriters

On the Job

How much should an insurance company charge for insurance? That depends on how likely a customer is to have an accident. Using national statistics, underwriters decide whether a person applying for insurance is a good risk. They also help the company decide how much to charge. If they set the rates too low, the company will lose money. Too high, and the company will lose business to competitors.

Subjects to Study

Math, statistics, economics, English, business courses, accounting

Discover More

Talk with an insurance agent in your community. Ask about the company's rates. Are rates higher for those under 21? Are there other groups the company considers high-risk? Do people who live downtown pay higher rates than those in the suburbs? Are rates higher for people who own sports cars or minivans? Why?

Related Jobs

Accountants and auditors; actuaries; budget analysts; cost estimators; financial analysts and personal financial advisors; financial managers; loan officers; insurance sales agents; claims adjusters, appraisers, examiners, and investigators

Education & Training
Bachelor's degree

Earnings
$$$$

Job Outlook
Little change

Loan Officers

On the Job

When you apply for a loan, you must provide information on your work, your assets and debts, and your credit rating. A loan officer will meet with you and help you fill out the application. Then he or she looks through your information and helps the bank decide whether to loan you the money; that is, the loan officer tries to predict whether or not you will pay it back.

Subjects to Study

Math, accounting, English, speech, computer skills, business courses, psychology

Discover More

Ask for a loan application from your parents' bank or credit union. Fill it out completely, including all of your sources of income, your savings, and your debts. Are you a good credit risk? Would you loan yourself money? Will your parents loan you money? And at what interest rate?

Related Jobs

Securities, commodities, and financial services sales agents; financial analysts and personal financial advisors; real estate brokers and sales agents; insurance sales agents

Education & Training
Bachelor's degree

Earnings
$$$$

Job Outlook
Little change

Management Analysts

On the Job

Companies hire management analysts to solve problems. The work varies with each client and from project to project. When a management team realizes there is a problem, it may call in a consultant to collect and review information, figure out where and why the problem is happening, and decide how to fix it. The job may require frequent traveling. Some management analysts work for consulting firms. Others are self-employed consultants.

SOMETHING EXTRA

Do you have what it takes to be a consultant? Many consultants are self-employed. They work on contract for a business, helping managers find the best way to solve a problem or make a product. When their work is done, they move on to the next client. Consultants must be detail-oriented, independent, and more than a little opinionated. They also should enjoy working on their own.

Subjects to Study

English, math, business courses, economics, accounting, journalism, speech

Discover More

Many consultants are self-employed. Interview people you know who are self-employed. How do they find their clients? Do they advertise? What do they like and dislike about being self-employed?

Related Jobs

Accountants and auditors; budget analysts; cost estimators; financial analysts and personal financial advisors; operations research analysts; economists; market and survey researchers; administrative services managers; financial managers; human resources, training, and labor relations managers and specialists; top executives

Education & Training
Bachelor's degree +

Earnings
$$$$$

Job Outlook
Above-average increase

Meeting & Convention Planners

On the Job

These planners are responsible for ensuring that meetings and conventions come off without a hitch. They coordinate every detail: arranging speakers and locations, acquiring the necessary equipment, and dealing with any problems that may arise. They interact with a variety of people and must have good communication skills. The job is fast paced and requires a great deal of energy and sharp organization skills.

Subjects to Study

English, math, business courses, speech, foreign languages

Discover More

Ask your teacher whether you can plan the next class function, or ask your parents whether you can plan their next party or social event. Draw up a schedule of activities and a list of resources you will need (food, beverages, entertainment, decorations). Coordinate every aspect of the event from the guest list to name tags and see whether you can plan a successful gathering.

Related Jobs

Food service managers; actors, producers, and directors; travel agents

Education & Training
Bachelor's degree

Earnings
$$$$

Job Outlook
Above-average increase

Tax Examiners, Collectors & Revenue Agents

On the Job

Tax examiners, collectors, and revenue agents work for the federal, state, and local governments. They review tax returns to make sure people and businesses are paying the right amount, send notices to those who have made mistakes, and track down those who are trying to avoid taxes altogether. Most work 40-hour weeks, except during tax season when overtime is common.

SOMETHING EXTRA

As far back as ancient Egypt, governments have been collecting taxes. Most ancient books, including the Torah, the Bible, and Hindu Sutras, mention paying taxes. Some kings collected animals, crops, or slaves from taxpayers; later governments demanded gold or jewels. Today, the IRS accepts money orders, personal checks, charge cards, or electronic fund transfers—but no sheep or corn!

Subjects to Study

Math, business courses, accounting, computer skills, English, foreign languages

Discover More

From January until April, your local library stocks tax forms of all kinds. Pick up a 1040 EZ form and ask your parents or a teacher to help you fill it out based on your allowance or job earnings. Read through all of the deductions carefully—you never know which ones you will qualify for!

Related Jobs

Accountants and auditors, budget analysts, cost estimators, financial analysts and personal financial advisors, financial managers, loan officers

Education & Training
Bachelor's degree

Earnings
$$$$

Job Outlook
Little change

Professional & Related Occupations

PHOTOGRAPHER

MATHEMATICIAN

CAN YOU READ THIS?

OPTOMETRIST

Actuaries

On the Job

Actuaries analyze risk. Most of them design insurance plans that will help their company make a profit. They study statistics and social trends to decide how much money an insurance company should charge for an insurance policy. They then predict the amount of money an insurance company will have to pay to its customers for claims. Some actuaries are self-employed and work as consultants.

Subjects to Study

Math, English, calculus, accounting, computer science

Discover More

Take a survey in your class. How many of your classmates have broken a bone or sprained an ankle? How many have stayed overnight in a hospital? How many have had their tonsils or appendix removed? Now separate the answers by boys and girls. Which group has had more medical emergencies? That's the group you would charge more for insurance.

Related Jobs

Accountants and auditors, budget analysts, economists, market and survey researchers, financial analysts and personal financial advisors, insurance underwriters, mathematicians, statisticians

Education & Training
Bachelor's degree +

Earnings
$$$$$

Job Outlook
Above-average increase

Computer Programmers

On the Job

Computer programmers write, update, test, and maintain the software that makes computers work. They provide detailed, step-by-step instructions for the computer. If the software does not produce the desired result, the programmer must correct the errors until the program works effectively. Some may work nights so that the computers are available to businesses during the day.

Subjects to Study

Computer science, math, physics, electronics

Discover More

The image you see on a computer monitor is made up of thousands of tiny dots. Color monitors use red, green, and blue dots. Use a magnifying glass to look at the screen, or use a drop of water to act like a lens. Get a tiny drop of water on your finger tip and touch it to your computer screen. (Be careful not to drip!) Do you see the dots?

Related Jobs

Computer software engineers, computer scientists and database administrators, computer systems analysts, mathematicians, engineers, statisticians, operations research analysts

Education & Training
Bachelor's degree

Earnings
$$$$$

Job Outlook
Little change

Computer Scientists & Database Administrators

On the Job

Computer scientists work as researchers and inventors. Some work for universities, while others work for research companies. Many work on cutting-edge technology such as virtual reality or robot design. Database administrators find ways to organize and store data. They work with large companies, maintaining the security and integrity of their computer networks. They work primarily in offices or laboratories.

Subjects to Study

Computer science, math, shop and technology courses, statistics

Discover More

What kinds of information backup systems does your school use? Ask your computer lab or media center specialist to show you the ways they store the information in the school's computers. Some back up the information onto other computers, but many simply use writable CDs or Zip disks to store material.

Related Jobs

Computer programmers, computer software engineers, computer and information systems managers, engineers, mathematicians, statisticians

Education & Training
Associate degree to Doctoral degree

Earnings
$$$$$

Job Outlook
Rapid increase

Computer Software Engineers

On the Job

Computer software engineers do research, design computers and programs, and find new ways to use them in business. They may identify problems in business, science, and engineering and then design specialized computer software to solve those problems. This kind of work can result in eyestrain, backaches, and hand and wrist problems.

SOMETHING EXTRA

Have you heard of carpal tunnel syndrome? It's a painful condition that occurs when tendons in the wrist become inflamed. The syndrome is common among people who do lots of work using computer keyboards. How do you avoid carpal tunnel syndrome? Try using a split keyboard or resting your wrists on a support while you type. Most important, if you must type for long periods of time, be sure to take frequent breaks.

Subjects to Study

Math, physics, computer science, communication skills, shop and technology courses

Discover More

Did you know your computer gives out radio waves? Try this experiment and see. Get a small radio and set it on AM. Turn it on and find a spot between stations so that you just receive static. Now turn the radio up high and put it next to your computer. You should hear sounds from your computer on the radio!

Related Jobs

Computer systems analysts, computer scientists and database administrators, computer programmers, computer support specialists and systems administrators, statisticians, mathematicians, engineers, actuaries

Education & Training
Bachelor's degree

Earnings
$$$$$

Job Outlook
Rapid increase

Computer Support Specialists & Systems Administrators

On the Job

What happens when a company's computers suddenly begin crashing? They call in the support specialist, the troubleshooters of the computer world. These workers find and fix problems for businesses and individual computer owners. Systems administrators help companies decide what kind of system they need; then they design, install, and support the organization's computer network. They may work overtime if problems arise.

Subjects to Study

Math, physics, computer science, shop and technology courses

Education & Training
Associate degree to Bachelor's degree

Earnings
$$$$

Job Outlook
Rapid increase

Discover More

Call the tech support hotline for a computer company. (Ask your parents first; these calls may cost money, and many are long-distance.) Ask how the support person can fix a computer problem over the phone.

Related Jobs

Computer programmers, computer software engineers, computer systems analysts, computer scientists and database administrators

Computer Systems Analysts

On the Job

Computer systems analysts are primarily responsible for assessing and meeting the technology needs of other businesses. They help businesses and organizations decide what computer systems will best help them grow or solve their problems. They often set up and test the new technology as well.

SOMETHING EXTRA

Computer software and hardware often becomes outdated almost as soon as you buy it. The average lifespan for a personal computer is two years, and nearly 6,000 computers become obsolete every day in California alone. Computer systems analysts have to be aware of these changes in technology so they can keep businesses on the cutting edge.

Subjects to Study

Math, physics, computer science, business courses, shop and technology courses

Discover More

Research the specifications and features of your computer at school or at home. How fast is the processor? How much RAM does it have? How big is the hard drive? What operating system is it running? Now compare it to one of the more expensive computers that just came on the market to see how outdated it is.

Education & Training
Bachelor's degree

Related Jobs

Computer programmers, computer software engineers, computer and information systems managers, computer scientists and database administrators, engineers, mathematicians, statisticians, operations research analysts

Earnings
$$$$$

Job Outlook
Rapid increase

Mathematicians

On the Job

Mathematicians work in two areas: theory and applications. Theoretical mathematicians look for relationships between new math principles and old ones. This can help in science and engineering.

Applied mathematicians use math to solve problems in business, government, and everyday life. Many mathematicians teach at colleges and universities.

Subjects to Study

Algebra, geometry, trigonometry, calculus, logic, computer science, physics, statistics

Discover More

To try your hand at some fun and challenging math activities, visit the MathCats at www.mathcats.com, or the Galileo gallery of math puzzles at www.galileo.org/math/puzzles.html.

Education & Training
Master's degree

Earnings
$$$$$

Related Jobs

Actuaries; statisticians; computer programmers; computer systems analysts; computer scientists and database administrators; computer software engineers; operations research analysts; teachers—postsecondary; teachers—preschool, kindergarten, middle, elementary, and secondary; engineers; economists; market and survey researchers; financial analysts and personal financial advisors; physicists and astronomers

Job Outlook
Declining

Operations Research Analysts

On the Job

Operations research analysts help businesses operate efficiently by applying mathematical principles to problems. First, analysts define and study the problem. Next, they gather information by talking with people and choosing which mathematical model they will use. Finally, they present their findings and recommendations to the company's management.

SOMETHING EXTRA

Airlines are famous for being late. To help them stay on time, operations research analysts set up schedules for flights and maintenance, estimate the number of passengers flying at different times, and decide how much fuel is needed for each flight. When you consider how many flights an airline runs each day, you can see what a big job that is. The wonder is that anyone ever gets anywhere on time!

Subjects to Study

Math, statistics, computer skills, English, communication skills, logic, business courses

Discover More

Take a walk through your school building. Now, using graph paper, make a map of the building, including all the classrooms, offices, restrooms, cafeteria, and exits. Using your map, plot the most direct, effective way to deliver mail to each classroom and office. Then plot the most efficient exit route from each classroom.

Education & Training
Master's degree

Related Jobs

Computer systems analysts, computer scientists and database administrators, computer programmers, engineers, mathematicians, statisticians, economists, market and survey researchers, computer and information systems managers, management analysts

Earnings
$$$$$

Job Outlook
Little change

Statisticians

On the Job

Statisticians collect information from surveys and experiments. They decide where and how to gather the information, who to survey, and what questions to ask. They use the information they collect to make predictions about the economy or to assess various social problems. This helps business and government leaders make decisions. Because computers play such a big role in collecting and analyzing data, statisticians need to know as much about computers as they do about math.

Subjects to Study

Math, algebra, statistics, economics, business courses, sciences, computer skills

Discover More

The next time you go to a sporting event like a football or baseball game, take a notebook and pen with you. Try to keep track of the statistics of one team or of key players. At the end of the game, add up your figures and provide a summary of the team's or players' performance.

Related Jobs

Mathematicians, operations research analysts, computer systems analysts, computer scientists and database administrators, computer programmers, computer software engineers, engineers, economists, market and survey researchers, computer and information systems managers, management analysts

Education & Training
Master's degree

Earnings
$$$$$

Job Outlook
Little change

Architects, Except Landscape & Naval

On the Job

Architects design buildings and other structures. They make sure buildings are functional, safe, and economical. They draw plans of every part of a building, including the plumbing and electrical systems. They also help choose a building site and decide what materials to use. Most architects today use computers in their work, and many are self-employed.

SOMETHING EXTRA

Architecture can be a tricky business. Take, for example, the bell tower for a certain cathedral in the Italian city of Pisa. Before it was even completed (in 1174), it began to lean—which is why the top section is still kinked. The Leaning Tower of Pisa has been leaning for more than 800 years now, and architectural engineers are still finding new ways to keep it propped up!

Subjects to Study

Math, English, drawing courses, drafting, computer science, shop and technology courses

Discover More

What does your dream house look like? Using graph paper, draw a room-by-room floor plan of your ideal home. Include all the elements you would like—maybe a fireplace, an exercise room, a game room, or a spa. Don't forget the practical rooms—everyone needs a kitchen and a bath!

Related Jobs

Construction managers, landscape architects, engineers, urban and regional planners, interior designers, commercial and industrial designers, graphic designers

Education & Training
Bachelor's degree

Earnings
$$$$$

Job Outlook
Average increase

Landscape Architects

On the Job

Landscape architects make areas such as parks, malls, and golf courses beautiful and useful. They decide where the buildings, roads, and walkways will go, and how the flower gardens and trees should be arranged. They create designs, estimate costs, and check that the plans are being carried out correctly. They also must make sure their designs are environmentally friendly. Some work for major companies, but many are self-employed.

Subjects to Study

Math, botany, ecology, drafting, art, geology, computer skills

Discover More

Design a flower garden that will grow in your area's climate. What colors do you want? Should you use tall plants, short ones, or a combination? Do you want all spring-bloomers or plants that will bloom at various times? Check catalogs and local nurseries for prices. How much will your garden cost? How much maintenance will it need?

Education & Training
Bachelor's degree

Earnings
$$$$$

Job Outlook
Above-average increase

Related Jobs

Architects, except landscape and naval; surveyors, cartographers, photogrammetrists, and surveying technicians; engineers; urban and regional planners; conservation scientists and foresters; biological scientists; medical scientists; environmental scientists and hydrologists; geoscientists

Surveyors, Cartographers, Photogram-metrists & Surveying Technicians

On the Job

These workers measure and map the earth's surface to set official land, air, and water boundaries. They may check old legal documents for information and write reports. They work outdoors in all kinds of weather and may travel long distances to work sites. Cartographers use the information surveyors gather to prepare maps and charts. Photogrammetrists analyze aerial photographs to help make detailed maps.

SOMETHING EXTRA

Satellites are changing the way surveyors work today. A "Global Positioning System" uses radio signals from satellites to locate points on the earth. The surveyor places a radio receiver at the desired point, and the receiver can collect information from several satellites at once. Such a receiver can also be placed in a car and used to trace a road system. And to think at one time we thought the world was flat!

Subjects to Study

Algebra, geometry, trigonometry, drafting, computer science, English, geography, geology, photography

Discover More

Make a map of your neighborhood, showing how to get from your house to your school. Include all streets and important landmarks, bodies of water or forests, malls or business districts, parks and playgrounds—anything that acts as a landmark in your area. If you gave someone at school your map, could the person get to your house?

Education & Training
Moderate-term OJT to Bachelor's degree

Earnings
$$$$

Related Jobs

Engineers; architects, except landscape and naval; landscape architects; environmental scientists and hydrologists; geoscientists; urban and regional planners

Job Outlook
Average increase

Engineers

On the Job

Engineers design machinery, buildings, and highways. They also develop new products and new ways of making them. Some engineers test the quality of products. Some supervise production in factories. They may work in laboratories, offices, and construction sites. Most engineers specialize to work in a particular industry or with particular materials, for example, aerospace engineers, agricultural engineers, chemical engineers, and mechanical engineers.

Subjects to Study

Math, physics, chemistry, shop and technology courses, drafting, computer skills

Discover More

You've probably made paper airplanes before, but have you experimented with your design in order to increase their flight? Have you tried using heavier or lighter paper, or different kinds of glue, or cut flaps in the wings? Using different designs and materials, make five different paper airplanes and do a series of test flights. What design worked best and why?

Education & Training
Bachelor's degree

Earnings
$$$$$

Job Outlook
Average increase

Related Jobs

Architects, except landscape and naval; engineering and natural sciences managers; computer and information systems managers; computer programmers; computer software engineers; drafters; engineering technicians; sales engineers; science technicians

Drafters

On the Job

Drafters prepare the drawings used to build everything from spacecraft to bridges. Using rough sketches done by others, they produce detailed technical drawings with specific information to create a finished product. Drafters use handbooks, tables, calculators, and computers to do their work. Many specialize in architecture, electronics, or aeronautics.

SOMETHING EXTRA

Why are blueprints blue? Before computer-aided drafting, drafters would place their original drawing over special chemically treated white paper. A bright light was shone on the combined sheets of paper for several minutes, and then the special treated paper was placed in a developing solution. The result: The paper turned blue everywhere except for where the original tracing had blocked the light, creating a perfect negative image of the original drawing—a blueprint!

Subjects to Study

Math, physics, drafting, art and design courses, computer skills, shop and technology courses

Discover More

Try making your own drawing of a building or some kind of machine. You can use either paper and pencil or a computer drawing program. You can find books about drafting at the library.

Related Jobs

Architects, except landscape and naval; landscape architects; commercial and industrial designers; engineers; engineering technicians; science technicians; surveyors, cartographers, photogrammetrists, and surveying technicians

Education & Training
Voc/tech training

Earnings
$$$$

Job Outlook
Little change

Engineering Technicians

On the Job

Engineering technicians use science, engineering, and math to solve problems for businesses. They help engineers and scientists with experiments and develop models of new equipment. Some supervise production workers or check the quality of products. Like engineers, they often specialize in an area such as mechanics, electronics, or chemicals. Some may be exposed to hazards from equipment, chemicals, or toxic materials.

Subjects to Study

Math, physics, chemistry, electronics, shop and technology courses, drafting

Discover More

What's the simplest way to boil an egg? Easy, right? Just put the egg in a pan of boiling water and cook it. Now think about the reverse. How *complicated* can you make the job? On paper, draw an egg-boiling machine. Make it as complicated and ridiculous as you can.

Related Jobs

Science technicians; drafters; surveyors, cartographers, photogrammetrists, and surveying technicians; broadcast and sound engineering technicians and radio operators

Education & Training
Associate degree

Earnings
$$$$

Job Outlook
Average increase

Agricultural & Food Scientists

On the Job

Agricultural scientists study farm crops and animals. They look for ways to control pests and weeds safely, increase crop yields with less labor, and save water and soil. They may specialize in plant, soil, or animal science. Many work outdoors in all kinds of weather. Food scientists work in the food processing industry, at universities, and for the government. They look for new food sources and preservatives and help ensure that our country's food supply is safe.

SOMETHING EXTRA

Will chickens hatch in space? Scientists wondered how the lack of gravity would affect hatching eggs, so they sent fertilized chicken eggs into space aboard the space shuttle. Some of the eggs did not survive the flight. Of the ones that survived, some eggs did hatch. The space chickens returned to Earth safe and sound (the astronauts took enough other food supplies with them) to be studied further.

Subjects to Study

Biology, environmental science, physics, chemistry, math, business, life sciences, nutrition, family and consumer sciences

Discover More

Set up a growing experiment of your own. Choose a plant and get a package of seeds at a garden center. Now plant the seeds in four containers. Put two containers on a sunny windowsill and two in a shady spot. Water one in the window and one in the shade every day. Water the other two only once every four or five days. Which seeds grow best?

Education & Training
Bachelor's degree

Earnings
$$$$$

Related Jobs

Biological scientists; chemists and materials scientists; conservation scientists and foresters; farmers, ranchers, and agricultural managers; veterinarians; landscape architects

Job Outlook
Average increase

Biological Scientists

On the Job

Biological scientists study living things and their environment. They do research, develop new medicines, increase crop amounts, and improve the environment. Some study specialty areas such as viruses, ocean life, plant life, or animal life. They may work in company, college, or government labs, or as high school biology teachers.

Subjects to Study

Math, biology, botany, chemistry, zoology, physics, computer science, environmental studies

Discover More

Study the effects of acid rain on plant life. Get two small potted plants from a garden center. Keep them in the same place. Water one daily with regular tap water. Water the other with "acid rain" you make by adding a half teaspoon of white vinegar to two and a half teaspoons of tap water. Which plant grows better?

Related Jobs

Medical scientists, agricultural and food scientists, conservation scientists and foresters, physicians and surgeons, dentists, veterinarians

Education & Training
Doctoral degree

Earnings
$$$$$

Job Outlook
Average increase

Medical Scientists

On the Job

Medical scientists research human diseases in order to improve human health. Most medical scientists do basic research to learn more about viruses, bacteria, and other infectious diseases. Then this information is used to develop vaccines, medicines, and treatments for many diseases. While some work in clinics or hospitals, most work in government, university, or private industry labs.

SOMETHING EXTRA

Did you know that people once thought smoking was good for you? Early TV ads promoted smoking cigarettes as a refreshing, healthy way to relax. It took medical scientists to prove that smoking puts people at risk for lung cancer and heart disease. Supplying information based on their research is one way medical scientists help people live longer, healthier lives.

Subjects to Study

Chemistry, biology, math, physics, computer science

Discover More

Take a walk in the woods or the park and look for piles of leaves and fallen tree limbs and sticks. Notice that at the bottom of the piles, the leaves and sticks have started to crumble and fall apart. What causes this? Special microbes such as bacteria eat up dead material such as leaves and sticks and turn it into a powder called compost. Take some of the compost home and put it on your houseplants or in your garden. Does it help your plants grow bigger?

Related Jobs

Biological scientists, agricultural and food scientists, physicians and surgeons, dentists, veterinarians

Education & Training
Doctoral degree

Earnings
$$$$$

Job Outlook
Rapid increase

Conservation Scientists & Foresters

SOMETHING EXTRA

In 1980, a volcano in Washington state called Mount St. Helens erupted, blowing off the entire north face of the mountain. The blast destroyed thousands of acres of forest and heated the ground so much that nothing grew for years. Rather than replanting, the U.S. Forest Service decided to leave the blast site alone, to watch how the mountain recovered on its own. Today, the first signs of life—wildflowers and saplings—are growing. In a hundred years or so, there will be a new forest.

On the Job

Foresters and conservation scientists manage, use, and protect natural resources such as water, wood, and wildlife. Foresters supervise the use of timber for lumber companies. Range managers oversee and protect range lands so that the environment is not damaged. Soil conservationists help farmers save the soil, water, and other natural resources. All of these workers spend time outdoors in all kinds of weather.

Subjects to Study

Math, chemistry, biology, botany, ecology, agriculture, computer science, economics, business courses

Education & Training
Bachelor's degree

Earnings
$$$$$

Job Outlook
Little change

Discover More

Foresters understand that for every tree that is cut down, a new tree must be planted. Ask your parents if you can pick out a tree from a local nursery and plant it in your yard, taking into consideration the tree's needs for sunlight and space. Or talk to your teachers at school about the possibility of organizing a tree planting event. For more information on how to plant trees, visit this Web site: www.kidsface.org/pages/plant.html.

Related Jobs

Engineers; agricultural and food scientists; biological scientists; environmental scientists and hydrologists; geoscientists; farmers, ranchers, and agricultural managers

Atmospheric Scientists

On the Job

Atmospheric scientists, commonly called meteorologists, study the atmosphere (the air that covers the earth) for its effects on our environment. The most well-known area of their work is weather forecasting. They also study trends in the earth's climate and apply their research to air-pollution control, environmental studies, air and sea transportation, and defense. Meteorologists often work nights, weekends, and holidays at weather stations.

SOMETHING EXTRA

Even with advanced warning from meteorologists, it is sometimes difficult to avoid the destruction that can be caused by Mother Nature. In late August of 2005 Hurricane Katrina hit in Florida, Mississippi, Alabama, and Louisiana, with particularly devastating effects on the city of New Orleans. Killing at least 1,600 people and doing $75 billion in damage, it is considered the most destructive hurricane in American history.

Subjects to Study

Math, chemistry, physics, computer science, statistics, environmental science

Discover More

Contact a local TV station in your area and ask to become one of its weather watchers. Hang a thermometer outside—a little way away from your home. Take daily readings. Place a large, rimmed dish on a flat surface outside to measure rain or snowfall. Call your reports in to the TV station and watch the weather report for your information.

Related Jobs

Environmental scientists and hydrologists, geoscientists, physicists and astronomers, mathematicians, engineers

Education & Training
Bachelor's degree

Earnings
$$$$$

Job Outlook
Average increase

Chemists & Materials Scientists

On the Job

Chemists and materials scientists look for and use new information about chemicals and other materials. They develop new paints, fibers, adhesives, drugs, and other products. They also develop processes that save energy and reduce pollution. They make improvements in agriculture, medicine, and food processing. Most work in manufacturing firms or teach at colleges and universities. Their line of work can be dangerous.

Subjects to Study

Math, physics, chemistry, biology, computer science, business courses

Discover More

Have you ever mixed Mentos and diet soda? First stack a dozen Mentos candies on top of one another, using paper or an index card to keep them stacked together. Open a full 2-liter bottle of diet soda. Then drop the roll of candies all at once into the bottle and stand back. You might want to do this outdoors as the resulting eruption can get messy.

Related Jobs

Agricultural and food scientists, biological scientists, medical scientists, engineers, physicists and astronomers, science technicians

Education & Training
Bachelor's degree

Earnings
$$$$$

Job Outlook
Little change

Environmental Scientists & Hydrologists

On the Job

Environmental scientists and hydrologists study the earth and humans' impact on it. Many are involved in water conservation and the preservation of natural resources. All of these scientists play an important role in maintaining a healthy environment, designing waste-disposal sites, and cleaning up polluted land and water.

SOMETHING EXTRA

The average family goes through about 70 gallons of water per day washing clothes and dishes, taking showers, and flushing toilets. Americans drink more than one billion glasses of tap water per day. This doesn't include the amount of water used to keep lawns green and flowers growing. These are just some of the reasons hydrologists are constantly searching for greater supplies of fresh water.

Subjects to Study

Math, computer science, chemistry, physics, geology

Discover More

You don't have to have a college degree to begin thinking of ways to help maintain the environment. Make a list of ten things you can do to help—such as turning off lights when you leave the room or buying recycled paper—and share the list with your parents, friends, and teachers.

Related Jobs

Conservation scientists and foresters; atmospheric scientists; science and engineering technicians; physicists; chemists; engineers; surveyors, cartographers, photogrammetrists, and surveying technicians

Education & Training
Master's degree

Earnings
$$$$$

Job Outlook
Above-average increase

Geoscientists

SOMETHING EXTRA

One of the hottest fields in geology is seismology—the study of earthquakes. And one of the biggest seismology experiments in history is still happening today in Parkfield, California. This small town is known for its regular pattern of earthquakes: For the last 150 years, Parkfield has experienced a magnitude 6 earthquake every 20 to 30 years. The latest struck in September of 2004, finally giving researchers there something to write about.

On the Job

Like environmental scientists and hydrologists, geoscientists also study the earth, though they focus on its composition and geologic history. Many are involved in the search for natural resources while others concern themselves with cleaning up the environment. Oceanographers study the world's oceans and coastal waters, and geologists study rock formation to learn more about the history of the Earth.

Subjects to Study

Math, computer science, chemistry, physics, geology

Discover More

Earthquakes happen when tectonic plates of the earth's surface move. You can see the same effect by cracking the shell of a hard-boiled egg. The thin shell represents the earth's crust, moving around on the slippery mantle. Move the pieces of shell around. What happens when they collide? Eggquake!

Related Jobs

Engineering technicians; science technicians; engineers; surveyors; cartographers, photogrammetrists, and surveying technicians; physicists and astronomers; chemists and materials scientists; atmospheric scientists; environmental scientists and hydrologists

Education & Training
Master's degree

Earnings
$$$$$

Job Outlook
Average increase

Physicists & Astronomers

On the Job

Physicists study the matter that makes up the universe. They also study forces of nature such as gravity, motion, and the nature of energy, electromagnetism, and nuclear interactions. They use their studies to design medical equipment, electronic devices, and lasers.

SOMETHING EXTRA

In the early 1940s, physicists working at a secret U.S. defense lab in Los Alamos, New Mexico, made a scientific breakthrough. They split an atom, setting off a chain of events that led directly to the atomic bombs dropped by the U.S. during World War II on Hiroshima and Nagasaki, Japan. Several of those scientists later regretted their work on the bomb. For better or worse, they assured their place in the history books and ushered in the atomic age.

Astronomers study the moon, sun, planets, galaxies, and stars. Their knowledge is used in space flight and navigation. Many teach in colleges and universities.

Subjects to Study

Math, physics, chemistry, computer science, geology, astronomy

Discover More

One of the easiest ways to begin to learn more about astronomy is to become an amateur star-gazer. Even without a telescope (though it certainly helps to have one, or at least a pair of binoculars), you can use a star chart to help you identify planets and constellations. Also listen to the news for special observation events like meteor showers or lunar eclipses.

Education & Training
Doctoral degree

Earnings
$$$$$

Related Jobs

Engineers, chemists and materials scientists, atmospheric scientists, environmental scientists and hydrologists, geoscientists, computer systems analysts, computer scientists and database administrators, computer programmers, mathematicians

Job Outlook
Little change

Economists

Interest is the extra fee that people pay for borrowing money from the bank. The amount of interest that people pay on loans for cars, houses, credit cards, and more changes from day to day. These interest rates are determined by the Federal Reserve Board and announced by its chairman. Because of this important power, even a whisper of activity by the Federal Reserve Board can cause the stock market to go up or down.

On the Job

Economists study how people use resources like land, labor, raw materials, and machinery to make products. They monitor inflation, interest rates, and employment levels. They use their studies to advise businesses and government agencies.

Subjects to Study

Math, English, economics, business courses, computer science, accounting

Discover More

Do you ever hear your parents complain about the rising price of gasoline? Keep track of the price of premium gas at your local station each day over the course of several weeks. Plot the price changes on a graph. Are there days each week when the prices are the highest? On days when the prices are higher, are there any related events in the news that might have caused the increase?

Education & Training
Master's degree

Earnings
$$$$$

Job Outlook
Little change

Related Jobs

Accountants and auditors; actuaries; budget analysts; financial analysts and personal financial advisors; financial managers; insurance underwriters; loan officers; purchasing managers, buyers, and purchasing agents; management analysts; market and survey researchers

Market and Survey Researchers

On the Job

Market and survey researchers tell businesses about the best ways to sell a product based on information they gather through interviews and questionnaires. Market research analysts might also develop advertising brochures and commercials, sales plans, and product promotions such as rebates and giveaways. Some analysts are self-employed and must travel to work for different clients.

SOMETHING EXTRA

A market researcher might spend her day on the telephone asking restaurants why they didn't buy more of a certain brand of crackers. Or she might invite groups of consumers to the office in the evening to test new products and give their opinions. Maybe you or your parents have been approached at the mall by someone with a clipboard wanting to ask your opinions. Market survey companies often have offices in malls because they can easily find lots of people to survey there.

Subjects to Study

Economics, psychology, English, sociology, math, statistics

Discover More

Take a survey in your class. Buy several different kinds of tortilla chips, then do a blind taste test: blindfold several classmates, then have them taste the chips. Keep a tally of which ones they prefer. Ask why they prefer one brand over another. These are the kinds of market surveys that researchers perform.

Related Jobs

Economists, psychologists, sociologists, statisticians, urban and regional planners

Education & Training
Master's degree

Earnings
$$$$$

Job Outlook
Above-average increase

Psychologists

On the Job

Psychologists study the way people think, feel, and act. They work to understand, explain, and change people's behavior. They may conduct training programs, do market research, or provide counseling. They may also work with mentally ill individuals. Psychologists work with schools, businesses, and health-care centers to help people deal with stress and changes in their lives, such as divorce and aging.

Subjects to Study

English, psychology, statistics, communication skills, biology, physical sciences, computer science

Discover More

Try this experiment: Get a small fish in a bowl. Feed it at the same time every day. Each time you feed the fish, just before you put the food in the water, tap on the side of the bowl. Soon, when your fish sees you tap on the bowl, it will look for food on the water's surface. That's called conditioning!

Related Jobs

Counselors, physicians and surgeons, social workers, teachers—special education

Education & Training
Master's degree to Doctoral degree

Earnings
$$$$$

Job Outlook
Above-average increase

Urban & Regional Planners

On the Job

Urban and regional planners develop programs that encourage growth in certain communities and regions. They make plans for the best use of land and study the area's schools, hospitals, parks, roads, and other facilities to see whether they meet the needs of the community. They also deal with legal codes and environmental issues, and a majority of them work for local governments. They often travel to inspect the features of the land to help in their planning.

> ### SOMETHING EXTRA
>
> Have you heard the term planned community? Whereas most cities simply grow as more people move in and open businesses, planned communities are plotted in detail before the first house is built. The Disney Corporation built a planned community in Florida that's made to look like an old-fashioned town. It's called Celebration, and it's an easy day's drive from Disney World (you know, in case you get bored at Disney World).

Subjects to Study

Math, English, speech, government, psychology, computer science, sociology, geography

Discover More

Plan a town on graph paper. Include all the roads, houses, schools, churches, and parks. Don't forget hospitals, police and fire stations, gas stations, sources for water and electricity, a shopping district, and a town center. A Starbucks is optional.

Related Jobs

Architects, except landscape and naval; engineers; landscape architects

Education & Training
Master's degree

Earnings
$$$$$

Job Outlook
Average increase

Social Scientists, Other

Have you seen any of the Indiana Jones movies? How about The Mummy? Think that's what archaeology is all about? Think again! Most archaeologists spend years researching their subjects before even beginning a major dig. Then months more are spent sifting through every artifact found, deciding what culture produced it and when. Of course, there are exciting moments. Imagine being the first human in 2,000 years to enter an ancient tomb and find gold. Just don't expect to dodge any rolling boulders.

On the Job

There are many kinds of social scientists. Anthropologists study the origins and development of human society, ancient ways of life, languages, tools, and archaeological remains around the world. Geographers study how physical geography affects politics and culture. Historians research and interpret the past. Political scientists study political systems and public policy. Sociologists study social behavior and groups as well as religious, political, and business organizations.

Subjects to Study

English, history, political science, sociology, mathematics, geography

Education & Training

Master's degree

Earnings

$$$$$

Job Outlook

Average increase

Discover More

Imagine it is the year 3,010 and anthropologists are studying humans from *our* day and age. How do you think they will describe us? What about our way of life, technology, culture, and beliefs will they find interesting, puzzling, or humorous? Write a couple of paragraphs analyzing our society from their point of view.

Related Jobs

Economists; lawyers; statisticians; news analysts, reporters, and correspondents; social workers; psychologists; teachers; counselors; archivists, curators, and museum technicians

Science Technicians

On the Job

Science technicians use science and math to solve research problems. They also investigate, invent, and help improve products. They set up, operate, and maintain lab equipment, monitor experiments, and record results. They may specialize in agriculture, biology, chemistry, or other sciences. Their work tends to be more practical in nature. Some work outdoors and may be exposed to chemicals or radiation.

SOMETHING EXTRA

Finding new uses for agricultural crops can be important to areas that grow those crops. George Washington Carver's work is an excellent example of this. Carver, the son of slaves, developed hundreds of uses for two Southern crops: the peanut and the sweet potato. His work helped the South's economy and made him a nationally recognized scientist.

Subjects to Study

Math, physics, chemistry, biology, geology, shop and technology courses, computer science

Discover More

Science technicians need good eye-hand coordination and a good ability to follow written instructions. You can hone your skills by putting together model cars or model ships. Are the directions in the kit clear and easy to follow? How would you change them to make them clearer?

Related Jobs

Engineering technicians, broadcast and sound engineering technicians and radio operators, drafters, clinical laboratory technologists and technicians, diagnostic medical sonographers, radiologic technologists and technicians

Education & Training
Associate degree

Earnings
$$$$

Job Outlook
Average increase

Counselors

On the Job

Counselors help people with their problems; the work they do depends on the people they serve. School counselors help students with personal, social, and behavioral problems. College placement counselors help students decide on careers and find jobs. Rehabilitation counselors help people with disabilities and addictions. Employment counselors help people decide what kinds of jobs they want and help them find work.

Subjects to Study

English, speech, psychology, social studies, sociology, computer skills, communication skills

Discover More

Talk to your school counselor about this job. What are the most difficult and most rewarding parts of the job? Find out what professional organizations he or she belongs to. Write to one of those organizations or visit their Web sites to learn more about counseling.

Related Jobs

Teachers; social and human service assistants; social workers; psychologists; physicians and surgeons; registered nurses; occupational therapists; human resources, training, and labor relations managers and specialists

Education & Training
Bachelor's degree to Master's degree

Earnings
$$$$

Job Outlook
Above-average increase

Probation Officers & Correctional Treatment Specialists

On the Job

Many people who are convicted of crimes are placed on probation instead of being sent to jail. Probation officers supervise these people, making sure they stay out of trouble. Correctional treatment specialists work with people in jails and prisons, evaluating their progress, planning special programs, and counseling offenders. All of these specialists work with criminal offenders, some of whom are dangerous.

SOMETHING EXTRA

What happens when a man commits a crime in Ohio but is captured in Florida? Or a woman is convicted in Utah but will serve her sentence in Illinois? Sometimes, prisoners are simply handcuffed and put on a regular airplane—with a guard, of course. But what about prisoners who are too dangerous for commercial flights? They have their own airline! The U.S. Marshals Service operates a fleet of planes they use to transport prisoners from one place to another. Imagine how tight security must be on those flights!

Subjects to Study

English, speech, psychology, social studies, criminal justice, sociology

Discover More

Call your state's Department of Corrections, explain your interest in the job, and ask to interview a probation officer. What are the best parts of the job? What are the worst? Does the officer work from 9 to 5, or is he or she on call 24 hours a day? You can get more information on this job from the American Probation and Parole Association at www.appa-net.org.

Related Jobs

Social workers, social and human service assistants, counselors, police and detectives, correctional officers

Education & Training
Bachelor's degree

Earnings
$$$$

Job Outlook
Average increase

Social & Human Service Assistants

Do you enjoy helping people? Do you have lots of patience? Do you spend time volunteering at school or in your community? Social service workers spend their days helping the elderly, the handicapped, children, and low-income families. Although the pay for these positions often is low, social service workers receive the reward of knowing they make a difference in someone's life each day.

On the Job

Social and human service assistants are in the business of helping people. They might work in a food bank, train mentally handicapped adults to do a job, or supervise groups of teenagers in a day program. They evaluate clients' needs, help them fill out the paperwork to get benefits, keep records, and file reports with social service agencies. They work in offices, hospitals, group homes, and private agencies.

Subjects to Study

English, speech, psychology, sociology, writing skills

Discover More

You can check out the social service field by volunteering at a food bank, an adult day-care center, a mental-health institution, or a community center in your neighborhood.

Related Jobs

Social workers; counselors; childcare workers; occupational therapist assistants and aides; physical therapy assistants and aides; nursing, psychiatric and home health aides

Education & Training
Moderate-term OJT

Earnings
$$

Job Outlook
Rapid increase

Social Workers

On the Job

Social workers work with people to help them find solutions to their problems. They might help a client find housing, a job, or health care. They deal with issues like child abuse, poverty, unplanned pregnancy, alcohol or drug abuse, and criminal behavior. They help people cope with serious illnesses and crisis situations. They may work in hospitals, social service agencies, group homes, government agencies, or schools.

SOMETHING EXTRA

Do people tell you you're a good listener? Do you enjoy helping your friends figure out solutions to their problems? If so, social work might be a good field for you. A social worker's job is never the same from day to day. On Monday, you might help an elderly client find affordable housing, on Tuesday counsel a pregnant teenager, and on Wednesday visit an abused child in a foster home. Like many jobs in social service, the rewards often come from knowing you helped others.

Subjects to Study

English, communication skills, psychology, biology, sociology, history, foreign languages

Discover More

Talk to the counselor at your school about this job. Ask about the training and the kinds of situations he or she deals with on a daily basis. Ask whether he or she can help you set up a peer-counseling service at your school.

Related Jobs

Counselors, probation officers and correctional treatment specialists, psychologists, social and human services assistants

Education & Training
Bachelor's degree to Master's degree

Earnings
$$$$

Job Outlook
Above-average increase

Court Reporters

On the Job

These workers put spoken words into writing. They make notes using shorthand or a stenotype machine, which prints shorthand. They also use audio recordings and computer voice translation software. They are often responsible for helping judges and attorneys access information. Sometimes they type as fast as 200 words per minute. Because they are the only ones recording what is being said, they must be accurate.

Subjects to Study

English, word processing, spelling, foreign languages, computer skills, communication skills

Discover More

Watch an actual court case on TV. Find the court reporter in the courtroom and watch what he or she does. Listen to all the statements made by the lawyers, witnesses, and judge. Try to imagine correctly recording every word they say.

Related Jobs

Secretaries and administrative assistants; medical transcriptionists; receptionists and information clerks; human resources assistants, except payroll and timekeeping; paralegals and legal assistants; data entry and information processing workers

Education & Training
Voc/tech training

Earnings
$$$$

Job Outlook
Average increase

Judges, Magistrates & Other Judicial Workers

On the Job

Judges, magistrates, and other judicial workers oversee trials and make sure that everyone follows the court rules. They preside over all types of cases, from traffic tickets to murder trials. In court cases without a jury, the judge decides the verdict. All judges work for the government, either local, state, or federal. Nearly all judges have law degrees.

SOMETHING EXTRA

Not all judges wear traditional black robes. In fact, judges both at the state and federal level are permitted to choose their own attire. Though most of them go for the basic black, there are some exceptions. Former Chief Justice of the Supreme Court William Rehnquist had four gold bars on the sleeves of his gown, supposedly inspired by an opera he saw. And the seven judges of the Maryland Court of Appeals wear red robes instead of black. A formal dress code is still implicit, of course, so you won't find judges in tank tops and flip-flops.

Subjects to Study

English, writing skills, public speaking, government, history, foreign languages, psychology, computer science, criminal justice

Discover More

Have a mock trial in your social studies class. Different students can be lawyers for the prosecution and the defense, the defendant, the witnesses, the jury, and the judge. The judge has the final say about what evidence can and cannot be presented.

Education & Training
Bachelor's degree +

Related Jobs

Counselors, lawyers, paralegals and legal assistants, private detectives and investigators

Earnings
$$$$$

Job Outlook
Average increase

Lawyers

Do you love to argue a point? Do you enjoy a good debate? Lawyers must be able to argue clearly and persuasively to convince the judge and jury of their points. But law isn't all about arguing. Lawyers spend hours researching their cases, questioning witnesses, looking for other cases that support their points, and studying the law. The brief flash in the courtroom is supported by lots of time in the library.

On the Job

Lawyers give people advice about the law and their rights. They represent people in court, presenting evidence that supports a client's position, asking questions, and arguing their case. Lawyers must do research to find the information they need to support their cases. They must have good reading, writing, and speaking skills. There are a number of areas that lawyers may specialize in from corporate to criminal law.

Subjects to Study

English, speech, government, history, foreign languages, psychology, computer skills, logic

Education & Training
Professional degree

Earnings
$$$$$

Job Outlook
Average increase

Discover More

Organize a class debate. Pick a topic you feel strongly about, take a position, and argue your side. Be sure you do some research first—read articles and books on the topic and find out what other people think of it. Can you change your opponents' minds?

Related Jobs

Paralegals and legal assistants; judges, magistrates, and other judicial workers

Paralegals and Legal Assistants

On the Job

Paralegals help lawyers prepare their cases. They do research and write reports that lawyers use to present their arguments in court. They may meet with clients to get information about a case, but they do not argue cases in court or set fees. Some paralegals have a wide variety of tasks, while others specialize in one area of the law, such as tax law or publishing law.

SOMETHING EXTRA

Paralegals today use computers to do their research. Special software packages and the Internet put a world of information at their finger tips. They simply enter a topic and receive a list of all documents on that subject. They also use computers to organize the volumes of paper needed to support cases. These programs help today's paralegals do in one day work that used to take weeks!

Subjects to Study

English, business courses, computer skills, foreign languages, logic

Discover More

Contact a law firm or a legal-aid society in your area. Ask to talk to a paralegal. Find out what his or her duties involve. Ask how he or she became interested in the occupation and what kind of training the job requires. Also feel free to visit this Web site hosted by the National Association of Legal Assistants: www.nala.org/whatis.htm

Related Jobs

Claims adjusters, appraisers, examiners, and investigators; occupational health and safety specialists and technicians

Education & Training
Associate degree to Bachelor's degree

Earnings
$$$$

Job Outlook
Above-average increase

Archivists, Curators & Museum Technicians

On the Job

These workers choose, buy, and care for collections of books, records, art, and other items for libraries and museums. The items might also include coins, stamps, plants, paintings, sculptures, or even animals. They may also work with records on paper, film, or computers. They plan exhibits, educational programs, and tours. Most work with the public and may travel to add to their collections.

Subjects to Study

English, speech, history, art, chemistry, physics, business courses, accounting

Discover More

Visit a museum or zoo in your area. Ask the tour guide about the collection. Who decides what to buy for the collection? Where do the exhibits come from? What would you like to see in the exhibit that's not already there?

Related Jobs

Artists and related workers; librarians; social scientists, other

Education & Training

Bachelor's degree to Master's degree

Earnings
$$$$

Job Outlook
Average increase

Instructional Coordinators

On the Job

Instructional coordinators develop teaching materials, train teachers, and assess school programs. They often specialize in a specific subject, such as language arts, math, or gifted and talented programs. Most work for school districts or independent consulting firms, and they spend time traveling between schools. The work can be stressful and involve long hours. Many instructional coordinators are former teachers and school administrators.

SOMETHING EXTRA

What happens when a school district's students aren't passing standardized tests? Most often, the district calls in a specialist to help research and solve the problem. As schools across the country place more and more emphasis on these tests, this job field is expected to grow rapidly. But keep in mind, the specialist is employed only as long as the district sees good results!

Subjects to Study

English, social sciences, business courses, psychology, computer science, foreign languages

Discover More

Call your school district's main offices and ask to interview the instructional coordinator or curriculum specialist. Does that person work only during the school year or year-round? What are the best and worst parts of the job?

Related Jobs

Teachers; education administrators; counselors; human resources, training, and labor relations managers and specialists

Education & Training
Master's degree

Earnings
$$$$

Job Outlook
Rapid increase

Librarians

On the Job

Librarians help people use the library and its materials. They help people find the books they need and fill out applications for library cards. They may give talks on how to use the library or read to children during special programs. Some manage other workers, prepare budgets, and order materials for their libraries. They may shelve books, update files, and design special displays. They must be very computer literate and keep up with changes in technology.

Subjects to Study

English, literature, accounting, social sciences, business courses, psychology, computer science

Education & Training
Master's degree

Earnings
$$$$

Job Outlook
Little change

Discover More

Take a tour of your school's library. Does your librarian order the books for your library? How does he or she decide which books to order? What guidelines does your school district provide? Ask whether you can look through the publishers' catalogs and circle some titles that look interesting to you.

Related Jobs

Archivists, curators, and museum technicians; teachers; computer and information systems managers; computer scientists and database administrators

Library Technicians

On the Job

Library technicians help librarians order, shelve, and organize library materials. They help people find materials and information. Some may also help maintain audiovisual equipment, prepare displays, and supervise other support staff. They answer questions, help patrons check out materials, and may send out notices to people with overdue books. Some work in school libraries, helping students find information they need for research.

SOMETHING EXTRA

What happens when you want a book your library doesn't have? You can order it through the interlibrary loan system. This means that your library borrows the book from another library, usually one in your state, and then loans the book to you. Your librarian can search the records of other libraries, find the closest one that has the book you want, and key in an order. In just a few days, the book is in your hands!

Subjects to Study

English, literature, accounting, computer skills, business courses

Discover More

Check your local library for volunteer opportunities. You might be put to work shelving books, helping at the checkout counter, supervising small children during reading programs, or straightening up at the end of the day.

Related Jobs

Library assistants, clerical; medical records and health information technicians

Education & Training
Short-term OJT

Earnings
$$

Job Outlook
Average increase

Teacher Assistants

On the Job

Teacher assistants help children in the classroom and school cafeteria or on the playground and field trips. Sometimes they pay special attention to individual students or small groups who need more help with a subject. They help teachers by grading papers, keeping attendance records, typing, filing, ordering supplies, helping out in the computer lab, or preparing class lessons.

Subjects to Study

English, communication skills, computer skills, math, foreign languages, speech, psychology

Discover More

Volunteer to help care for younger children at your school, church, or a local day-care center or youth organization. You might help them with schoolwork, play games, or teach a craft.

Related Jobs

Teachers—preschool, kindergarten, elementary, middle, and secondary; teachers—special education; librarians; childcare workers; library technicians; library assistants, clerical; occupational therapist assistants and aides

Education & Training
Short-term OJT

Earnings
$$

Job Outlook
Average increase

Teachers—Adult Literacy & Remedial Education

On the Job

Adult literacy and remedial education teachers teach basic skills courses—writing, reading, and math—to adults and out-of-school youths. They also work with people who want to update their job skills or prepare for the GED exam. An increasing number teach English as a second language to non-native speakers. Many work part-time, at night, or on the weekends.

SOMETHING EXTRA

Did you know that a significant portion of the adult population in the U.S. cannot read or struggles to read? Even people who graduate from high school sometimes have trouble reading. This makes it very hard to get and hold a job, to pay bills, or even to get a driver's license. Without reading skills, it's nearly impossible to get ahead in today's society.

Subjects to Study

English, communication and writing skills, math, social sciences, foreign languages

Discover More

Contact your local library about literacy programs they are currently running and ask whether they need volunteers. They may have you read stories to younger kids or become a reading tutor for someone learning the language.

Related Jobs

Teachers—preschool, kindergarten, elementary, middle, and secondary; teachers—special education; counselors; social workers

Education & Training
Bachelor's degree

Earnings
$$$$

Job Outlook
Average increase

Teachers—Postsecondary

On the Job

Postsecondary teachers work at colleges, community colleges, universities, and research facilities. They specialize in one field, such as history, physics, or journalism. They do research and write articles and books about their findings. Most professors hold advanced degrees. While many schools do not hold classes during the summer months, faculty still work year-round, preparing lectures, attending seminars, and conducting research.

SOMETHING EXTRA

Picture a university professor. Do you think of a white-bearded, bespectacled man lecturing in a big classroom? Today's college and university faculty are young and old, men and women, of every ethnic and racial background (though some of them still wear tweed coats). And they do more than lecture. Most are involved in some kind of original research in their field. If you love to learn about new ideas and then teach them to others, this might be the job for you.

Subjects to Study

English, math, speech, sciences, social sciences, foreign languages, computer science

Education & Training
Work experience to Professional degree

Discover More

Visit a college campus and sit in on a class or two. Watch the professor and think about how the class resembles or differs from your classes at school. Talk to the professor after class and ask about the job.

Earnings
$$$$$

Related Jobs

Teachers—preschool, kindergarten, elementary, middle, and secondary; education administrators; librarians; counselors; writers and editors; public relations specialists; management analysts

Job Outlook
Rapid increase

Teachers—Preschool, Kindergarten, Elementary, Middle & Secondary

On the Job

Teachers help students learn in school. They plan lessons, prepare tests, grade papers, and write reports of students' progress. They meet with parents and school staff to talk about grades and problems. Some teach a specific grade; others teach one subject to students in many grades.

Most work more than 40 hours a week, and some work second jobs during the summer months. Many supervise school activities such as clubs and sports teams.

SOMETHING EXTRA

Think about the challenges of being a working parent. You have to find someone to watch your kids while you are at work. This is hard enough during the school year, but in the summers and on Christmas break, it's especially tough. One of the things many teachers like about teaching is that they get the same days off as their kids. This cuts down on child-care costs and lets them plan vacations and activities for the whole family.

Subjects to Study

English, social studies, math, sciences, psychology, foreign languages, computer science

Discover More

Talk with your school counselor about programs such as peer tutoring or cadet teaching in your school. You can help younger students who are having trouble with a subject or grade papers for a teacher.

Related Jobs

Teachers—postsecondary; counselors; teacher assistants; education administrators; librarians; childcare workers; public relations specialists; social workers; athletes, coaches, umpires, and related workers

Education & Training
Bachelor's degree

Earnings
$$$$

Job Outlook
Above-average increase

Teachers—Self-Enrichment Education

On the Job

Self-enrichment teachers usually know a lot about a certain subject and are willing to share what they know with students (mostly adults) who are eager to learn. They may teach classes in cooking, literature, art, financial planning, spirituality, or any number of other topics. Most self-enrichment classes are informal and are designed for individuals who just want to improve themselves, enrich their lives, or just learn more about a topic.

Subjects to Study

English, social studies, social sciences, computer science, art, dance, physical education

Education & Training
Work experience

Discover More

Call a local community college or high school and ask for the catalog of continuing-education courses. Find a class that interests you, then call the school and ask whether you can sit in on a session of that class

Earnings
$$$$

Related Jobs

Teachers—preschool, kindergarten, elementary, middle, and secondary; dancers and choreographers; artists and related workers; musicians, singers, and related workers; recreation workers; athletes, coaches, umpires, and related workers

Job Outlook
Above-average increase

Teachers—Special Education

On the Job

Special education teachers work with students who have disabilities. Most work in elementary, middle, or high schools, but some work with toddlers and preschoolers. They prepare classes to meet their students' needs, grade papers, and write reports. They may teach academic studies or life skills. They meet with parents, counselors, school psychologists, and occupational or physical therapists to come up with the best school plan for each student.

Subjects to Study

English, social studies, math, sciences, psychology, foreign languages, computer science, art, dance, physical education

Discover More

Arrange with your teacher to spend a day observing a special education class at your school. Watch how the teacher interacts with the students. You might be able to help out by reading to younger children or tutoring them.

Related Jobs

Psychologists; social workers; speech-language pathologists; audiologists; counselors; teacher assistants; occupational therapists; recreational therapists; teachers—preschool, kindergarten, elementary, middle, and secondary

Education & Training
Bachelor's degree

Earnings
$$$$

Job Outlook
Above-average increase

Artists & Related Workers

On the Job

Artists use a variety of methods and materials to communicate through art. They might use oil paints, watercolors, pencils, clay, chalk, or even scrap metal to create their work. Visual artists are usually called graphic artists or fine artists. Graphic artists use art to meet the needs of business clients, such as stores, ad agencies, and publishing firms. Fine artists create artwork to sell and display in museums or galleries. More than half are self-employed and must use good business skills to be successful.

Subjects to Study

Art, drawing, drafting, computer skills, English, business courses

Discover More

The best way to prepare for this career is to take art classes, visit museums, study the styles of other artists, and practice, practice, practice.

Related Jobs

Architects, except landscape and naval; archivists, curators, and museum technicians; commercial and industrial designers; fashion designers; floral designers; graphic designers; interior designers; landscape architects; photographers; woodworkers; computer software engineers; desktop publishers

Education & Training
Long-term OJT to Bachelor's degree +

Earnings
$$$$$

Job Outlook
Average increase

Commercial and Industrial Designers

On the Job

These individuals are responsible for the look, feel, function, quality and safety of most of the products we use everyday. They combine knowledge of art, engineering, and business to create sketches and models that are then used in production. Often commercial and industrial designers specialize in one product or another, from automobiles to furniture. They are sometimes involved in testing and marketing products as well, and many of them are self-employed.

SOMETHING EXTRA

One of the more famous stories of industrial design actually concerns Post-it Notes—those little colored pieces of paper you see all over desks and offices. A researcher at 3M set out to make a stronger adhesive but ultimately only developed a weaker one that just barely stuck. Three years later, a fellow researcher at the company discovered he could coat scraps of paper with the stuff and use them as bookmarks. They would stick, but could be lifted off with ease. Now they are everywhere.

Subjects to Study

Art, drawing, drafting, business courses, English, computer skills

Discover More

On paper, design a brand-new minivan or sports car. Be sure to design both the exterior and interior. Will it have fold-down seats? A navigation system? Where will people put their cups? What kind of wheel rims do you want? Don't forget the safety features. Check out automobile magazines for ideas.

Related Jobs

Artists and related workers; architects, except landscape and naval; engineers; landscape architects; drafters; computer software engineers; desktop publishers; fashion designers; graphic designers; interior designers

Education & Training
Bachelor's degree

Earnings
$$$$$

Job Outlook
Average increase

Fashion Designers

On the Job

Fashion designers create the clothing, shoes, and accessories worn by billions of people. They research fashion trends, sketch designs, select materials, create prototypes, and oversee the production of their items. Some even work designing costumes for movies, television, and plays. Well over half of all fashion designers work in either California or New York.

Subjects to Study

Family and consumer sciences, art, drawing, business courses, English, computer skills

Education & Training
Bachelor's degree

Earnings
$$$$$

Job Outlook
Little change

Discover More

Talk to your teacher and principal about having a fall or spring fashion show. Head a committee to help with the planning, including choosing styles, models, and music. Charge a small entrance fee and give the proceeds to a local charity.

Related Jobs

Artists and related workers; commercial and industrial designers; floral designers; graphic designers; interior designers; demonstrators, product promoters, and models; photographers; purchasing managers, buyers, and purchasing agents; retail salespersons; textile, apparel, and furnishing occupations

Floral Designers

On the Job

Floral designers select flowers, greenery, ribbons, and containers and produce arrangements for decoration and special occasions. Most work independently or in small shops doing designs for special events like weddings and funerals. Others work in the wholesale floral business or in the floral departments in grocery stores. Floral designers often work under deadlines (the flowers need to be fresh, after all).

SOMETHING EXTRA

The average cost for flowers at a wedding range from $500 to $1,500. If that sounds like a lot, it helps to put it into context: The average total bill for a wedding is $22,000. The good news for floral designers is that people will continue to get married despite the cost, so there will always be a market for their services.

Subjects to Study

Botany, biology, family and consumer sciences, art, business courses, English

Discover More

If you have a flower garden at home, ask your parents whether you can pick a selection of them and make a table arrangement (be sure to ask for a vase as well). Alternatively, go to the grocery store and select a bouquet with a variety of flowers. Take it home and separate each stem; then make your own original arrangement instead.

Related Jobs

Artists and related workers, commercial and industrial designers, fashion designers, graphic designers, interior designers, landscape architects

Education & Training
Moderate-term OJT

Earnings
$$

Job Outlook
Average increase

Graphic Designers

On the Job

Otherwise known as graphic artists, these designers decide the best way to communicate a message in print, film, or electronic format. Some graphic designers develop the layout of newspapers and magazines, while others work in advertising on packaging and marketing materials. Perhaps the hottest trend in graphic designing is developing material for Web pages. Graphic designers are expected to be familiar with the latest computer design software.

Subjects to Study

Art, drawing, drafting, business courses, English, computer skills

Discover More

On paper, create a new logo for your school. You might want to create a new mascot and motto as well. Consider how the logo might appeal to parents, students, and teachers alike. What colors look best together? What overall message do you want the new logo to send? Where in the school would you expect to see it?

Related Jobs

Artists and related workers; commercial and industrial designers; fashion designers; floral designers; interior designers; computer software engineers; drafters; desktop publishers; advertising, marketing, promotions, public relations, and sales managers; photographers; writers and editors

Education & Training
Bachelor's degree

Earnings
$$$$

Job Outlook
Average increase

Interior Designers

On the Job

Interior designers are responsible for designing and arranging the physical space within a building, whether it's a home, hospital, theater, restaurant, or office. They experiment with colors, textures, furniture, lighting, and space to create a safe, functional, and pleasing atmosphere. More and more often they are involved in planning the layouts of buildings as well.

SOMETHING EXTRA

Perhaps you have heard of Feng Shui. This ancient Chinese practice stems from Taoism and is concerned with achieving harmony with your surroundings. Through a careful arrangement of space, it is believed you can increase the flow of positive energy. Though originally based on a combination of philosophy and scientific calculation, it has recently been viewed as both a fad and a superstition in the United States.

Subjects to Study

Art, business courses, English, computer skills, family and consumer sciences, shop courses

Discover More

On paper, redesign a room of your home. Check out magazines for ideas. Get paint and wallpaper samples from the hardware store. Will you recover the furniture in new fabric? Hang new drapes? Replace the flooring? Decide on a color scheme and draw the room.

Related Jobs

Artists and related workers; architects, except landscape and naval; commercial and industrial designers; fashion designers; floral designers; graphic designers; landscape architects

Education & Training
Bachelor's degree

Earnings
$$$$

Job Outlook
Average increase

Actors, Producers & Directors

On the Job

Actors, producers, and directors make words come alive through plays, TV shows, and films. Actors play characters, speaking the lines written in the script and adding their own movements. Directors choose plays and scripts, select the actors, and conduct rehearsals for productions. Producers arrange the financing and decide the size of the production and the budget. Directors and producers often work under tight deadlines and stressful conditions.

Subjects to Study

English, speech, drama, music, dance, art, photography, business courses

Discover More

You can learn more about the theater by auditioning for a role in a school or community play. If being on stage is not for you, try working backstage, making props, working the lights or sound system, or helping with costumes and makeup.

Education & Training
Long-term OJT to Bachelor's degree +

Earnings
$$$$$

Related Jobs

Announcers; dancers and choreographers; musicians, singers, and related workers; writers and editors; fashion designers; top executives

Job Outlook
Average increase

Athletes, Coaches, Umpires & Related Workers

On the Job

From football to ice skating, professional athletes train every day to stay in top physical condition for competition. Coaches organize, lead, teach, and referee indoor and outdoor games such as volleyball and soccer. Some also teach specific skills, such as weight training, tennis, and gymnastics. Umpires make sure everyone follows the rules and sometimes have to make tough decisions. All of these jobs are very competitive.

SOMETHING EXTRA

Do you have what it takes to be a professional athlete? The answer, sadly, is probably not. Here are the facts: Every year in America, roughly 1 million young men play high school football; another 500,000 play basketball and baseball. How many make it to the pros? To put it in perspective, consider this: Only about 2 out of every 10,000 high school athletes ever sign a professional sports contract. Here's another sobering statistic: The average professional sports career lasts just four years.

Subjects to Study

Physical education, nutrition, biology, anatomy, sports education

Discover More

Participate in sports or physical-fitness activities at your school or local gym or YMCA. Take classes in an activity that interests you, then ask whether you can be a team member, team manager, or coach's assistant.

Related Jobs

Dietitians and nutritionists; physical therapists; recreation workers; fitness workers; recreational therapists; teachers—preschool, kindergarten, elementary, middle, and secondary

Education & Training
Long-term OJT

Earnings
$$$

Job Outlook
Above-average increase

Dancers & Choreographers

On the Job

Dancers express ideas and stories through the movement of their bodies. Dance styles include classical ballet, modern dance, tap, jazz, and different folk dances. Dancers perform in musicals, operas, TV shows, movies, music videos, and commercials. Dancers must be strong, coordinated, and dedicated. Choreographers create dances and teach dancers. They may work for one company or on a freelance basis. Those who operate their own studios must have good business skills.

Subjects to Study

Music, dance, physical education, drama, English, history

Education & Training
Long-term OJT to Work experience

Earnings
$$$$

Job Outlook
Average increase

Discover More

Sign up for dance classes at a local studio. Try several styles, from ballet to tap to swing. Ask the teacher about the job. Does he or she work at another job in addition to teaching? Does he or she perform with a dance company? Be sure to attend dance performances as well.

Related Jobs

Actors, producers, and directors; musicians, singers, and related workers; fashion designers; barbers, cosmetologists, and other personal appearance workers; athletes, coaches, umpires, and related workers

Musicians, Singers & Related Workers

On the Job

Musicians and singers play instruments and perform vocal music. They may perform alone or in groups, before live audiences or in recording studios. Composers write original songs for bands, orchestras, or singers. Conductors lead musical groups such as orchestras, dance bands, and ensembles. Most musicians work nights and weekends and must travel to perform. Because it's so hard to support themselves with music, many take other jobs as well. Many musicians work in cities with recording studios, such as New York, Los Angeles, and Nashville.

SOMETHING EXTRA

Did you ever wonder what famous musicians did before they were famous? Some, like Britney Spears, hit it big early, but others had to work their way up from obscurity. Garth Brooks, for instance, beefed up as a nightclub bouncer while waiting to be discovered. Mariah Carey worked nights as a janitor in a beauty salon. As for Madonna—the ultimate material girl— she did counter duty at the Times Square Dunkin' Donuts.

Subjects to Study

Vocal music, instrumental music, English, creative writing, business courses

Discover More

Participate in your school band, orchestra, or choir. Audition for a role in a school or community musical. Take lessons to learn a musical instrument.

Related Jobs

Precision instrument and equipment repairers; actors, producers, and directors; announcers; dancers and choreographers

Education & Training
Long-term OJT to Master's degree

Earnings
$$$$

Job Outlook
Average increase

Announcers

On the Job

Radio announcers (or disc jockeys) plan and perform radio programs. They may choose and play music, interview guests, and write program material. Television announcers and newscasters prepare and present the news, weather, and sports, although most specialize in one of these areas. They may work unusual hours, including very early in the morning and very late at night. When emergency situations arise, they must be there to cover them for the news.

Subjects to Study

English, public speaking, drama, foreign languages, electronics, computer skills

Education & Training

Moderate-term OJT to Associate degree

Earnings

$$

Job Outlook

Declining

Discover More

Ask the principal at your school if you can make the morning announcements one day. Write out your "intro" and try to make it humorous or catchy. Can you entertain your audience members while you keep them informed? That's the job of an announcer.

Related Jobs

News analysts, reporters, and correspondents; interpreters and translators; actors, producers, and directors; musicians, singers, and related workers; broadcast and sound engineering technicians and radio operators; public-relations specialists; writers and editors

Broadcast & Sound Engineering Technicians & Radio Operators

On the Job

Broadcast and sound engineering technicians work with electronic equipment to record and transmit radio and television programs. They operate, install, and repair microphones, TV cameras, tape recorders, and antennas. They often work holidays, weekends, and evenings for news programs. When disasters happen, they must be on the scene to record the news. Setting up equipment sometimes requires heavy lifting and climbing.

SOMETHING EXTRA

Did you ever wonder how a moviemaker got a certain sound—maybe the hum of a spacecraft engine or the blast of a star exploding? The soundtrack in a movie is made by sound mixers, using everything from explosives to cabbage to corn flakes. Using a process called dubbing, sound mixers sit at a console facing the movie screen and add the special-effect sounds and music. The sounds are then mixed on one master tape, which becomes the movie's soundtrack.

Subjects to Study

Math, shop courses, physics, electronics, English, computer skills

Discover More

Build your own electronic equipment using a hobby kit. Check a toy or hobby store to see what kind of equipment is available. Operating a "ham" or amateur radio is great experience for this occupation.

Related Jobs

Engineering technicians, science technicians, electrical and electronics installers and repairers, computer support specialists and systems administrators, communications equipment operators

Education & Training
Moderate-term OJT to Associate degree

Earnings
$$$$

Job Outlook
Average increase

Interpreters and Translators

SOMETHING EXTRA

Did you know that one out of every five Americans speaks a language other than English at home? That's more than 50 million people who speak Spanish, Chinese, French, German, Russian, or some other language. So imagine the growing need for people who can translate and interpret between English and these languages. Many businesses and government agencies have an urgent need for translators to help them communicate with their customers.

On the Job

Interpreters and translators convert spoken and written words from one language into another. These language specialists also relay concepts and ideas between languages. They must thoroughly understand the subject about which they are translating. They also need to be sensitive to other cultures. This work can be sporadic, and many interpreters and translators work part time.

Subjects to Study

English, speech, foreign languages, computer skills

Discover More

The United Nations is an assembly of representatives from countries all over the world. The UN's job is to maintain international peace and security, to develop friendly relations among nations, to help solve international problems, and to promote human rights and freedoms. Its headquarters in New York employs many translators. Learn more about the UN at www.un.org/Pubs/CyberSchoolBus.

Education & Training
Long-term OJT

Earnings
$$$$

Job Outlook
Above-average increase

Related Jobs

Teachers, announcers, writers and editors, computer software engineers, court reporters, medical transcriptionists

News Analysts, Reporters & Correspondents

On the Job

News analysts, reporters, and correspondents gather information and write articles or deliver reports about events around the world. Some take photographs or shoot videos. Radio and television reporters often report "live" from the scene of crimes or disasters. The work is usually hectic and stressful and the deadlines are tight. Reporting can be dangerous work and requires long hours, irregular schedules, and lots of travel.

SOMETHING EXTRA

Though it might seem glamorous at times to be in front of the camera, reporters and correspondents are often called upon to do dangerous work. Though every precaution is taken to ensure their safety, war correspondents often find themselves in potentially deadly situations. The war in Iraq, begun in March of 2003, had claimed the lives of 67 journalists three years later, nearly the same number of journalists as were killed in the Vietnam conflict.

Subjects to Study

English, journalism, social studies, history, creative writing, speech, computer skills, foreign languages

Discover More

Collect three or more newspapers that are all reporting on the same story. Read the reports and then make notes about how each newspaper's story differs from the others. The facts may be the same, but one paper may choose to play up sensational aspects while another pushes a different viewpoint.

Related Jobs

Writers and editors, public relations specialists, announcers, interpreters and translators

Education & Training
Bachelor's degree

Earnings
$$$$

Job Outlook
Little change

Photographers

On the Job

Photographers use cameras to record people, places, and events on film. Most specialize in commercial, portrait, or journalistic photography. Commercial photographers may take school or wedding pictures or photos for ads. Portrait photographers work in studios, taking pictures of people for special occasions. Journalistic photographers work for newspapers and magazines.

Subjects to Study

English, journalism, photography, art, creative writing, business courses

Discover More

Take photos of special people and places in your life. Try using different kinds of film and different lenses. For example, use black-and-white film to photograph your neighborhood. Use a telephoto lens to take pictures of small flowers and insects. Create a portfolio of what you consider to be your best work and show it around.

Related Jobs

Architects, except landscape and naval; artists and related workers; commercial and industrial designers; fashion designers; graphic designers; news analysts, reporters, and correspondents; television, video, and motion picture camera operators and editors

Education & Training
Long-term OJT

Earnings
$$$

Job Outlook
Average increase

Public Relations Specialists

On the Job

Public relations specialists work to present a good image of their clients to the public. Their job is to make sure the clients' good news is spread far and wide and to put a positive "spin" on bad news. They write press releases and speeches and set up "photo opportunities" of their clients doing good things. Many work more than 40 hours a week. In an emergency, they may be on call around the clock.

SOMETHING EXTRA

Who takes the heat head-on when there's a scandal in the White House? If you answered "the president," you've never seen a White House news conference. The press secretary is the link between the White House and the world. When scandal strikes, it's the press secretary who faces reporters, answers questions, and tries to defuse the situation. Former press secretaries often refer to the position as "the toughest job in the world."

Subjects to Study

English, creative writing, journalism, psychology, sociology, computer skills, speech, foreign languages

Discover More

Write a weekly press release for your class, announcing some good news or interesting event. Be sure the release is honest but puts forth the best possible image. Keep it short and snappy to be sure it gets attention!

Related Jobs

Advertising, marketing, promotions, public relations, and sales managers; demonstrators, product promoters, and models; news analysts, reporters, and correspondents; lawyers; market and survey researchers; sales representatives, wholesale and manufacturing

Education & Training
Bachelor's degree

Earnings
$$$$

Job Outlook
Above-average increase

Television, Video & Motion Picture Camera Operators & Editors

On the Job

Camera operators work behind the scenes on TV shows, documentaries, motion pictures, and industrial films. They shoot the film you see on screen, sometimes from high up on scaffolding or flat on their bellies on the ground. They may work long, irregular hours in places all over the world. Film editors look at the hundreds of hours worth of film shot for a project and decide which scenes to include and which to cut to produce the final product.

Subjects to Study

English, journalism, photography, art, business courses, electronics

Education & Training

Moderate-term OJT to Bachelor's degree

Earnings

$$$$

Job Outlook

Average increase

Discover More

Use a digital camcorder to make your own movie. These cameras let you load your movie onto a computer and then alter the images in countless ways. Give your leading lady green hair, edit in an explosion or two, drop in a few aliens, and make your own science-fiction flick.

Related Jobs

Artists and related workers, broadcast and sound engineering technicians and radio operators, photographers, graphic designers

Writers & Editors

On the Job

Writers write novels and non-fiction books, articles, scripts, plays, poems, and ads. They must also be able to sell what they have written. Editors choose the stories and books that publishing houses will print. Magazine editors choose articles for publication and assign stories to writers. Many of them also write stories and articles. Editors also review, rewrite, and correct the work of writers. Technical writers write training manuals, catalogs, assembly instructions, and project proposals.

SOMETHING EXTRA

So you want to be a writer, but you can't find time to write? Next time you feel that way, consider Anthony Trollope. This English novelist in the 1800s worked full time at the post office, yet managed to write dozens of books that are still in print today. How did he find the time? He wrote by the clock—producing a set number of pages every day. Trollope once wrote, "Three hours a day will produce as much as a man ought to write." So unless you have two full-time jobs, there should be nothing stopping you.

Subjects to Study

English, creative writing, journalism, computer skills, history, psychology

Discover More

Submit a story to a local newspaper or magazine. Check out *The Writer's Market* for those publications that encourage young writers, such as *Stone Soup*. You could also enter a writing contest.

Related Jobs

News analysts, reporters, and correspondents; interpreters and translators; announcers; public relations specialists

Education & Training
Bachelor's degree

Earnings
$$$$

Job Outlook
Average increase

Audiologists

On the Job

Audiologists work with people who cannot hear as well as they should. They use audiometers, computers, and other testing devices to diagnose hearing and balance disorders. They recommend treatments such as hearing aids, implants, or surgery. They work in hospitals, nursing homes, and schools. Those who work in private practice also must have good business sense.

Subjects to Study

English, math, physics, chemistry, biology, psychology

Discover More

You have probably had a hearing test at school. The next time hearing tests are being done at your school, ask the nurse or other person giving the test to tell you more about it. How does it measure hearing loss? What happens if a student is found to have a hearing loss?

Related Jobs

Occupational therapists, optometrists, physical therapists, psychologists, recreational therapists, counselors, speech-language pathologists

Education & Training
Master's degree

Earnings
$$$$$

Job Outlook
Average increase

Chiropractors

On the Job

Chiropractors help people who have problems with their muscles, nerves, or skeleton, especially the spine. They examine patients, order tests, and take X rays. They treat patients by massaging or adjusting the spinal column. They also use water and heat therapy. They stress nutrition, exercise, and reducing stress in treatment. They do not prescribe drugs or perform surgery. Many are self-employed.

SOMETHING EXTRA

What does a chiropractor have to do with treating headaches? As it turns out, quite a lot. Headaches can result from poor posture, tension, or a misalignment of the spinal cord. Using massage, heat therapy, and realignment exercises and techniques, chiropractors can help people who suffer from persistent or chronic headaches. They also teach people how to prevent headaches in the first place, which might be the best treatment of all.

Subjects to Study

Health, biology, anatomy, nutrition, chemistry, physics, psychology, math

Discover More

Aromatherapy is the practice of using different smells to relax, calm, or energize yourself. Try an experiment at home. Buy several different scented candles. Each evening at dinner, light a different candle. (Get your parents' permission first!) How do the different scents affect your mood (or your appetite)?

Related Jobs

Athletic trainers, massage therapists, occupational therapists, physical therapists, physicians and surgeons, podiatrists, veterinarians

Education & Training
Professional degree

Earnings
$$$$$

Job Outlook
Above-average increase

Dentists

Dentists have been practicing for nearly 7,000 years, although you might not recognize some of the treatments used back then as dentistry. In ancient Babylon, for example, "dentists" used worms, prayers, and herbs to treat tooth decay. In the Middle Ages, dentists were considered the first surgeons—although about all they could do was remove teeth, which they did to treat nearly every condition you can think of.

On the Job

Dentists help people take care of their teeth. They remove teeth and straighten them with braces, repair broken teeth, and fill cavities. They may replace a patient's original teeth with a "bridge" of false teeth. They may also perform surgery to treat gum disease. They teach people how to brush, floss, and care for their teeth to prevent problems. They wear masks, gloves, and safety glasses to protect themselves from infectious diseases. Many are self-employed.

Subjects to Study

Biology, anatomy, chemistry, physics, health, math, business courses

Discover More

The next time you visit your dentist—and before you have to open wide—ask him or her about the job. What kind of training is available in your area? What is the best part of the job? What's the worst? Is your dentist bothered that so many people are afraid of dentists?

Education & Training
Professional degree

Earnings
$$$$$

Related Jobs

Chiropractors, optometrists, physicians and surgeons, podiatrists, psychologists, veterinarians

Job Outlook
Average increase

Dietitians & Nutritionists

On the Job

Dietitians and nutritionists plan, prepare, and serve meals in clinics, schools, nursing homes, and hospitals. They help prevent and treat illnesses by teaching clients to eat properly. Some specialize in helping overweight or critically ill patients, or in caring for kidney or diabetic patients. Those supervising kitchen workers may be on their feet most of the day in a hot, steamy kitchen. Some are self-employed and act as consultants.

SOMETHING EXTRA

What's your favorite food? Is it a healthy, low-fat salad, or a big, greasy burger with fries? The food we eat affects our lives in countless ways. Currently about 65% of American adults are overweight, and bad eating habits can lead to obesity, low energy and fatigue, diabetes, heart disease, and certain kinds of cancer. Learning to eat healthy foods now will make a huge difference in your life today and tomorrow.

Subjects to Study

Health, nutrition, family and consumer sciences, biology, chemistry, English, accounting

Discover More

Plan and help prepare a healthy, low-fat meal for your family for each day of the week. Be sure to include grains, fruits, vegetables, dairy products, and foods high in protein.

Related Jobs

Food service managers, registered nurses

Education & Training
Bachelor's degree

Earnings
$$$$

Job Outlook
Above-average increase

Occupational Therapists

On the Job

Occupational therapists help people with disabilities become independent and productive. They may help a patient learn to use a wheelchair or work on a new skill. They also help patients find jobs and develop job skills. They usually work in hospitals, schools, or rehab centers. Some provide home health care. The job can be tiring, and therapists must sometimes lift patients and move heavy equipment.

Subjects to Study

Biology, chemistry, physics, health, art, psychology, English, foreign languages

Discover More

Volunteer at a local nursing home to help with activities. You might teach a stroke victim to knit, read to a person whose sight is fading, or simply visit someone whose family is far away.

Education & Training
Bachelor's degree

Related Jobs

Audiologists, chiropractors, physical therapists, recreational therapists, respiratory therapists, speech-language pathologists

Earnings
$$$$$

Job Outlook
Rapid increase

Optometrists

On the Job

Optometrists examine people's eyes to diagnose vision problems and eye diseases. They prescribe glasses and contact lenses and treat certain eye disorders. Some optometrists work especially with the elderly or children. Others develop ways to protect workers' eyes from on-the-job strain or injury. Many are self-employed and work evenings and weekends to meet their patients' schedules.

SOMETHING EXTRA

We all know that in the future (if the movies are right) we will be using lasers to zap each other. But medical professionals are already using lasers to treat patients. In LASIK eye surgery, doctors use a laser to vaporize a portion of your cornea—the clear covering over the front of your eye—to reshape it, ultimately resulting in clearer vision.

Subjects to Study

Physics, chemistry, biology, anatomy, psychology, speech, math

Discover More

With your teacher, contact a local optometrist and ask him or her to visit your school, talk about the job, and do a basic vision screening.

Related Jobs

Chiropractors, dentists, physicians and surgeons, podiatrists, psychologists, veterinarians

Education & Training
Professional degree

Earnings
$$$$$

Job Outlook
Above-average increase

Pharmacists

A big part of a pharmacist's job is answering questions. Because pharmacists work with the public, these might range from "Can I take this cold remedy with this pain reliever?" to "How do I get rid of this wart?" Their special knowledge makes them the expert for patients and doctors alike. In fact, several cases have been reported of pharmacists catching doctors' errors, often with life-saving effects.

On the Job

Pharmacists measure and sell medication to people who are sick when a doctor says they need it. They must know about the correct use, composition, and effects of drugs. They tell patients about medicines, including reactions and possible side effects, and answer questions. Those in hospitals and clinics advise doctors and nurses on drugs and their effects. Most pharmacists spend much of the workday on their feet. They may wear gloves and safety masks when working with drugs. Many work nights and weekends.

Subjects to Study

Math, biology, chemistry, physics, social sciences, English, foreign languages

Education & Training
Professional degree

Earnings
$$$$$

Job Outlook
Above-average increase

Discover More

Talk to a pharmacist and ask about the training needed for this job. Ask how he or she keeps up with new drugs that hit the market every day. Then, just for fun, ask about the most ridiculous question he or she has ever been asked on the job.

Related Jobs

Pharmacy technicians, pharmacy aides, biological scientists, medical scientists, chemists and materials scientists, physicians and surgeons

Physical Therapists

On the Job

Physical therapists work with accident victims, stroke patients, and people with disabilities. They evaluate patients and make plans to help them recover their physical abilities and relieve pain. They may use electricity, heat, or cold to relieve pain, reduce swelling, or increase flexibility. They work in hospitals, clinics, and private offices. Physical therapists must be strong enough to move patients and heavy equipment.

SOMETHING EXTRA

Have you ever heard the term passive exercise? It's not some new weight-loss miracle; it's simply a way physical therapists can help patients who have not been able to move their muscles for a long time. The therapist stretches the patient's joints and muscles to build flexibility. Gradually, the patient begins to move his or her own muscles. The patient can then begin to exercise with weights.

Subjects to Study

Biology, chemistry, physics, psychology, anatomy, English, foreign languages

Discover More

Talk to the gym teacher at your school about this kind of work. Ask him or her to help you put together an exercise plan to help you build your own strength and endurance.

Related Jobs

Audiologists, chiropractors, occupational therapists, recreational therapists, counselors, respiratory therapists, speech-language pathologists

Education & Training
Master's degree

Earnings
$$$$$

Job Outlook
Rapid increase

Physician Assistants

SOMETHING EXTRA

In many small, rural communities in the United States, medical doctors are in short supply. Some communities have no resident doctors at all. In such communities, physician assistants (PAs) are the primary health care providers. They see patients on a day-to-day basis, handling routine office visits. A doctor visits the clinic one or two days a week, though the PA can call the doctor for advice or in emergencies.

On the Job

Physician assistants always work under the supervision of a physician. They handle many of the routine but time-consuming tasks physicians do, such as taking medical records, examining patients, and ordering X rays and tests. They also treat minor injuries. They often work weekends and evenings, and may make house calls or go to nursing homes to check on patients. Physician assistants are usually on their feet for long periods of time.

Subjects to Study

Biology, chemistry, math, psychology, English, foreign languages, anatomy, nutrition

Education & Training
Bachelor's degree

Earnings
$$$$$

Job Outlook
Rapid increase

Discover More

To learn more about this job, check out the Web site of the American Academy of Physician Assistants: www.aapa.org/geninfo1.html.

Related Jobs

Audiologists, occupational therapists, physical therapists, registered nurses, speech-language pathologists

Physicians & Surgeons

On the Job

Physicians help people who are sick or have been hurt. They examine patients, perform tests, prescribe treatments, and teach people about health care. Surgeons perform operations on patients with life-threatening illness and injuries. Physicians work in hospitals, clinics, and private practice. Many work 60 hours a week or more. They may be on call for emergency visits to the hospital. Most doctors must travel frequently from their offices to hospitals to care for patients.

SOMETHING EXTRA

When a woman goes into labor in the middle of the night, who does she call? Her doctor! Obstetricians often work as part of a group practice so that they can share the work of delivering babies who arrive after hours and on weekends and holidays. Each night of the week, a different doctor is on call to deliver babies and handle emergencies. That way, obstetricians get some nights to spend at home with their own families.

Subjects to Study

Physics, chemistry, biology, psychology, health, nutrition, English, math

Discover More

Call your local hospital and ask about volunteer opportunities. Many have programs that let young people visit with or read to patients, deliver packages, greet visitors, and help with the library cart.

Related Jobs

Chiropractors, dentists, optometrists, physician assistants, podiatrists, registered nurses, veterinarians

Education & Training
Professional degree

Earnings
$$$$$

Job Outlook
Above-average increase

Podiatrists

On the Job

Podiatrists diagnose and treat diseases and injuries of the foot and lower leg. They may treat corns, calluses, ingrown toenails, bunions, and arch problems. They also treat ankle and foot injuries, deformities, and infections. They take care of foot problems caused by diseases such as diabetes. They prescribe medications and order physical therapy. They set broken bones and perform surgery. Podiatrists usually run their own small businesses, but they may also visit patients in nursing homes and perform surgeries at hospitals.

Subjects to Study

Biology, chemistry, physics, anatomy, health, English

Discover More

For more information on this job, see the careers section of the Web site for the American Podiatric Medical Association: www.apma.org/careers.htm.

Related Jobs

Athletic trainers, chiropractors, massage therapists, occupational therapists, physical therapists, physicians and surgeons

Education & Training
Professional degree

Earnings
$$$$$

Job Outlook
Average increase

Radiation Therapists

On the Job

Radiation therapists use machines to administer radiation treatment to cancer patients. The machines project high-energy X rays that shrink and sometimes destroy cancerous cells. Therapists advise patients and perform the treatment. They most often work in hospitals and cancer treatment centers. Great care is taken to prevent overexposure to the radiation.

SOMETHING EXTRA

Cancer is the cause of death for nearly 500,000 people per year and more than a million new cases are discovered each year as well, according to the American Cancer Society. Yet most cancers are preventable with exercise and a healthy diet, not to mention routine checkups. And of course, it pays not to smoke, as a third of cancer cases are the result of tobacco use.

Subjects to Study

English, anatomy, psychology, physics, chemistry, biology

Discover More

To learn more about radiation therapy and the work therapists perform, visit the National Cancer Institute's Web site at www.cancer.gov/cancerinfo/radiation-therapy-and-you.

Related Jobs

Radiation technologists and technicians, diagnostic medical sonographers, nuclear medicine technicians, dental hygienists, respiratory therapists, registered nurses, physicians and surgeons.

Education & Training
Associate degree

Earnings
$$$$$

Job Outlook
Above-average increase

Recreational Therapists

SOMETHING EXTRA

Are you a natural-born party planner? How about putting your gift to work to help people? Activities directors in nursing homes plan fun activities for the residents. They might teach crafts, arts, or woodworking; organize sing-alongs; bring in outside groups for special programs; or invite residents' families and friends to a special dinner or a picnic on the lawn.

On the Job

Recreational therapists help people with medical problems improve their health and well-being. They teach patients games, arts and crafts, dance, music, and sports activities. These activities help patients regain skills they've lost because of illness or injury and improve their state of mind. They work closely with medical staff in hospitals and nursing homes. They must be strong enough to move patients and equipment and to participate in activities.

Subjects to Study

English, speech, communication skills, anatomy, psychology, health, art, music, dance, physical education

Discover More

Volunteer some time each week at a nursing home in your neighborhood. Ask the activities director whether you can help him or her plan and carry out activities for the residents. You might help with an art project, read to a patient, or call out numbers in the Bingo game.

Related Jobs

Occupational therapists, physical therapists, recreation workers

Education & Training
Bachelor's degree

Earnings
$$$$

Job Outlook
Little change

Registered Nurses

On the Job

Registered nurses care for the sick and injured and help people stay well. In clinics, hospitals, and nursing homes, they provide much of the day-to-day care for patients, under a doctor's supervision. They take patient histories, give shots and medicines, and teach patients about helping with their own care. Some assist in surgeries. Nurses work nights, weekends, and holidays, and they often work long shifts. They must be able to cope with emergencies and high stress.

SOMETHING EXTRA

You might know that nurses help doctors, but did you know that if you have surgery, your life might depend on one? According to several studies, hospitals with more registered nurses have lower death rates following surgeries than those with fewer nurses. That's because it's often a nurse who notices if a patient has a bad reaction to a drug or complications from surgery. It's a fact: Nurses save lives.

Subjects to Study

Health, biology, chemistry, physics, anatomy, psychology, nutrition, English, foreign languages

Discover More

One of the best ways to learn about working in the medical field is to volunteer at a hospital or nursing home. You might organize activities, visit with patients, deliver supplies, or help with basic patient care.

Education & Training
Associate degree

Related Jobs

Emergency medical technicians and paramedics; licensed practical and licensed vocational nurses; massage therapists; medical and health services managers; nursing, psychiatric, and home health aides; occupational therapists; physical therapists; physician assistants; respiratory therapists; social workers

Earnings
$$$$$

Job Outlook
Rapid increase

Respiratory Therapists

On the Job

Respiratory therapists care for patients with breathing problems, from premature babies to heart attack victims. They perform tests, connect patients to machines that help in breathing, and teach patients how to use these machines at home. Therapists may also help in surgery by removing mucus from a patient's lungs so that he or she can breathe more easily. Those in hospitals spend most of their time on their feet. They must be able to work calmly in emergencies.

Subjects to Study

Health, biology, chemistry, anatomy, physics, English

Discover More

Asthma is on the rise in the United States, especially among children. Talk to someone who has asthma and find out what type of medicine or therapy he or she uses to prevent or treat asthma attacks.

Related Jobs

Registered nurses, occupational therapists, physical therapists, radiation therapists

Education & Training
Voc/tech training to Associate degree

Earnings
$$$$

Job Outlook
Above-average increase

Speech-Language Pathologists

On the Job

Sometimes called speech thera-pists, speech-language pathol-ogists work with people who cannot speak well. They teach patients how to improve their language skills. They may teach sign language to non-speaking patients, and they also work with people who have swallow-ing difficulties. Some conduct research on how people communicate.

SOMETHING EXTRA

People who stutter often can speak and sing more smoothly when they speak as part of a group, as in a choir or when reciting the Pledge of Allegiance. Scien-tists used this fact to invent a device that helps people who stutter. It looks like a small hearing aid that is worn in the ear. The aid makes it sound to the person like he or she is speaking in a group, so he or she can speak more fluently.

Subjects to Study

English, foreign languages, speech, biology, chemistry, physics, psychology

Discover More

Speech therapists help clients learn to speak clearly. Practice your speaking skills by recording yourself while reading. Play back the recording and listen to your speaking skills. Are you clear and understandable? If not, practice speaking in front of a mirror and watch how you make the sounds.

Education & Training
Master's degree

Related Jobs

Audiologists, occupational therapists, optometrists, physical therapists, psychologists, recreational therapists

Earnings
$$$$$

Job Outlook
Average increase

Veterinarians

On the Job

Veterinarians care for pets, farm animals, zoo residents, and laboratory animals. They set broken bones, treat injuries, prescribe medicine, perform surgery, and vaccinate animals against diseases. They teach people how to care for animals. Most veterinarians treat animals in private clinics or hospitals and work 50 hours or more a week. They may work nights and weekends. Those treating large animals travel to farms or ranches to see their patients. A number of veterinarians engage in research.

Subjects to Study

Biology, chemistry, physics, zoology, English

Education & Training
Professional degree

Discover More

Visit an animal shelter and talk to the workers about volunteer opportunities. Some shelters let volunteers come in to feed, bathe, play with, and pet the animals.

Earnings
$$$$$

Related Jobs

Chiropractors, dentists, optometrists, physicians and surgeons, podiatrists, biological scientists, medical scientists, animal care and service workers, veterinary technologists and technicians

Job Outlook
Average increase

Athletic Trainers

On the Job

Athletic trainers specialize in the prevention and treatment of injuries to muscles and bones, most often related to injury playing sports, training, or exercising. They are also heavily involved in the rehabilitation process. They work in hospitals and clinics, but also with college and professional sports teams. Many of them work long hours, and night and weekend work is common.

SOMETHING EXTRA

Injuries are common in sports—there simply is no avoiding them. Sprains and strains, bruises and scrapes are a dime a dozen, but the more serious injuries can often be avoided with the proper training and equipment. The two most common sites for sports injuries are the ankles and knees. Thus it is always important to have the right shoes, guards, and braces, and not to overstress your body by pushing too hard.

Subjects to Study

Health, physical education, biology, anatomy, physics, chemistry

Discover More

If your school has sports teams, it probably has an athletic trainer that it consults in case of injury or for education. See if you can interview that person and ask him or her what training was required for the job.

Related Jobs

Emergency medical technicians and paramedics, physical therapists, physician assistants, registered nurses, licensed practical and licensed vocational nurses, recreational therapists, occupational therapists, respiratory therapists

Education & Training
Bachelor's degree

Earnings
$$$$

Job Outlook
Rapid increase

Cardiovascular Technologists & Technicians

On the Job

Cardiovascular technologists and technicians help doctors treat heart and blood vessel diseases. They use a variety of tests, monitor the results, prepare patients for procedures, and sometimes assist in surgery. They may schedule patient appointments, type doctors' reports, keep patient files, and care for the testing equipment. They usually work in hospitals and clinics and may work evenings and weekends.

Subjects to Study

Shop courses, communication skills, math, computer skills, health, biology, anatomy

Discover More

Talk to an EKG supervisor or a cardiologist at your local hospital. Ask a technician about on-the-job training opportunities in your area. The hospital staff can tell you more about this job.

Related Jobs

Diagnostic medical sonographers, nuclear medicine technologists, radiation therapists, radiologic technologists and technicians, respiratory therapists

Education & Training
Associate degree

Earnings
$$$$

Job Outlook
Rapid increase

Clinical Laboratory Technologists & Technicians

On the Job

These workers do medical tests to help detect, diagnose, and treat diseases. They match blood types, test for drug levels, and look for abnormal cells. They analyze test results and send them back to doctors. Special equipment allows them to do more than one test at a time. They may work nights and weekends. They wear gloves and masks to protect themselves from infections and diseases.

SOMETHING EXTRA

Cancer is a deadly disease, but today's screening tests are helping doctors win the war against this killer. Pap smears detect cervical cancer, mammograms find breast cancer, and biopsies help determine whether suspicious tissues are cancerous. After the doctor administers the test, he or she sends it to a lab for analysis. It is the lab technician who tests the samples and decides whether they are cancerous. These workers are in the business of saving lives.

Subjects to Study

Biology, chemistry, physics, computer skills, math

Discover More

Rub slices of white bread against different surfaces: a trash can, your hair, the inside of your desk, the floor, dirt, whatever. Seal each piece in a plastic bag with a label telling what it touched. Let the bags sit for a week, then look at them through a magnifying glass. Which surface generated the most mold? (Important: When you're finished, throw the bags away without opening them. Mold can make you sick!)

Related Jobs

Chemists and materials scientists, science technicians, veterinary technologists and technicians

Education & Training
Associate degree to Bachelor's degree

Earnings
$$$$

Job Outlook
Above-average increase

Dental Hygienists

On the Job

Dental hygienists examine patients' teeth and gums to find disease. They help dentists by cleaning patients' teeth, taking and developing X rays, and applying fluoride treatments. They teach patients how to brush and floss their teeth correctly. Many work part-time for more than one dentist, and they often work on weekends and evenings. They wear gloves and masks to protect themselves from diseases.

Subjects to Study

Biology, chemistry, health, nutrition, anatomy, English, foreign languages

Discover More

Dentists contend that flossing is just as important as brushing and recommend doing it at least once a day. Take an anonymous survey of your class and other classes, asking how often people brush and floss their teeth. The results might surprise you. Better yet, they might make you want to become a dental hygienist.

Related Jobs

Dental assistants, medical assistants, occupational therapist assistants and aides, physical therapist assistants and aides, physician assistants, registered nurses

Education & Training
Associate degree

Earnings
$$$$$

Job Outlook
Rapid increase

Diagnostic Medical Sonographers

On the Job

Sonographers use special machines that send sound waves through the body to diagnose illness. Doctors use the results of these tests to find tumors, check growing fetuses, and make medical decisions. Sonographers are on their feet for long periods and may have to lift patients. Most work normal hours, although they may be on call for emergencies.

SOMETHING EXTRA

Ultrasounds are very helpful in determining whether a pregnant woman is carrying more than one baby. These images show twins, triplets, and sometimes more fetuses growing inside. Imagine Bobbi McCaughey's surprise in 1997 when an ultrasound revealed seven babies! Mrs. McCaughey was the first woman in recorded history to deliver live septuplets, but her record was short lived as Nkem Chukwu of Texas delivered octuplets only a year later.

Subjects to Study

Health, biology, math, shop courses, computer science, English

Discover More

To learn more about sonography, visit an obstetrician's office and ask to watch an ultrasound. The sonographers use the machine to actually "see" inside a womb and show images of a growing baby. You might need them to point out key features like eyes and fingers as they go.

Related Jobs

Cardiovascular technologists and technicians, clinical laboratory technologists and technicians, nuclear medicine technologists, radiologic technologists and technicians, respiratory therapists

Education & Training
Associate degree

Earnings
$$$$$

Job Outlook
Rapid increase

Emergency Medical Technicians & Paramedics

On the Job

Emergency medical technicians (EMTs) and paramedics drive ambulances and give emergency medical care. They determine a patient's medical condition at the scene, stabilize the patient, then drive him or her to the hospital. They work outdoors in all kinds of weather, and the work can be very stressful. Some patients may become violent, and EMTs may be exposed to diseases. They are often on call and work long hours any day of the week.

Subjects to Study

Driver's education, health, biology, chemistry, anatomy, English, foreign languages

Education & Training
Voc/tech training

Earnings
$$$

Job Outlook
Rapid increase

Discover More

Check with the Red Cross in your area to register for a first-aid or CPR course. You can learn how to save another person's life and be helpful in different kinds of emergencies.

Related Jobs

Air traffic controllers, firefighting occupations, physician assistants, police and detectives, registered nurses

Licensed Practical & Licensed Vocational Nurses

On the Job

Licensed practical nurses (LPNs) take care of sick and injured people. They are supervised by doctors or registered nurses. They help patients with bathing, dressing, and personal hygiene; feed them; and care for their emotional needs. They keep their patients as comfortable as possible. Licensed vocational nurses (LVNs) are the same as LPNs, except that they are licensed to work in California and Texas. Nurses must be strong enough to lift patients and able to deal with stress.

SOMETHING EXTRA

Some LPNs work as private-duty nurses. Instead of working for a hospital or clinic, these nurses provide in-home care to patients. They may work 8 to 12 hours a day caring for a single patient. In some cases, their duties involve caring for other members of the patient's family as well. At night, most return to their own homes and families, but some actually live with their patients' families while they provide care.

Subjects to Study

Health, anatomy, psychology, first aid, nutrition, family and consumer sciences, English, foreign languages

Discover More

Licensed practical nursing courses are offered in some high school vocational programs. Talk to your school counselor about these programs and find out whether any are available through high schools in your area.

Related Jobs

Emergency medical technicians and paramedics; medical assistants; nursing, psychiatric, and home health aides; registered nurses; social and human service assistants; surgical technologists

Education & Training
Voc/tech training

Earnings
$$$$

Job Outlook
Average increase

Medical Records & Health Information Technicians

On the Job

These workers organize and keep track of patients' medical records. First, they make sure all the right forms have been signed. Then they put the information into a computer file. Finally, they code the information so that it can be pulled up easily. They may work day, evening, or night shifts. Health information technicians must be computer literate and pay close attention to details.

Subjects to Study

English, math, computer skills, anatomy, biology

Discover More

The American Health Information Management Association offers an independent-study program for health information technicians. You can write to the association at 919 N. Michigan Ave., Suite 1400, Chicago, IL 60611, or check out its Web site: www.ahima.org.

Education & Training
Associate degree

Earnings
$$$

Related Jobs

Medical transcriptionists

Job Outlook
Rapid increase

Nuclear Medicine Technologists

On the Job

Nuclear medicine technologists give radioactive drugs to patients. These drugs help doctors diagnose and treat diseases. Using a camera, the technologist follows the drug as it enters the patient's body and records the drug's effects using magnetic resonance imaging (MRI). Technologists must keep accurate, detailed patient records. Technologists must also be careful to keep from being exposed to too much radiation. They wear badges that measure radiation levels.

Subjects to Study

Biology, chemistry, physics, math, computer science

Discover More

You can get more information about this job by writing to the Joint Review Committee on Educational Programs in Nuclear Medicine Technology, #1 2nd Avenue East, Suite C, Polson, MT 59860-2320, or visit their Web site at www.jrcnmt.org.

Related Jobs

Cardiovascular technologists and technicians, clinical laboratory technologists and technicians, diagnostic medical sonographers, radiation therapists, radiologic technologists and technicians, respiratory therapists

Education & Training
Associate degree

Earnings
$$$$$

Job Outlook
Above-average increase

Occupational Health & Safety Specialists & Technicians

On the Job

These workers help keep workplaces safe and workers healthy. Nearly half work for federal, state, or local government agencies to enforce rules on health and safety. The rest work for companies to ensure that their workplaces are operating safely. They identify hazardous conditions and practices and make recommendations for fixing them. They also check that dangerous materials are stored and used properly.

Subjects to Study

Biology, chemistry, physics, geology, English, computer science

Education & Training

Associate degree to Master's degree

Earnings

$$$$

Job Outlook

Average increase

Discover More

Government health and safety specialists use rules established by the Occupational Safety and Health Administration (OSHA), part of the U.S. Department of Labor. You can learn more about OSHA from its Web site: www.osha.gov.

Related Jobs

Construction and building inspectors, correctional officers, financial examiners, fire inspectors, police and detectives

Opticians, Dispensing

On the Job

Dispensing opticians work for eye doctors, making glasses and contact lenses according to the doctors' orders. They also keep customer records, track inventory, and help customers find frames that fit them well. Many work evenings and weekends or part-time. They must be careful with the glass-cutting machinery and chemicals they use to make lenses.

SOMETHING EXTRA

When was the first eye surgery performed? Would you guess this century? Or in the 1800s? How about in 1000 B.C.? Long before glasses were invented, ancient surgeons were removing cataracts from people's eyes. Evidence indicates that this surgery was being performed in India more than 3,000 years ago—and probably without anesthesia!

Subjects to Study

Physics, anatomy, algebra, geometry, mechanical drawing

Discover More

Visit an optical store in your community. Look through the wide selection of eyewear and decide which frames best fit you. Use the opportunity to talk to one of the dispensing opticians about this job.

Related Jobs

Jewelers and precious stone and metal workers, precision instrument and equipment repairers

Education & Training
Long-term OJT

Earnings
$$$

Job Outlook
Average increase

Pharmacy Technicians

On the Job

Pharmacy technicians help licensed pharmacists provide medicines and other health-care products to patients. In pharmacies they help measure and prepare medications, handle telephone calls, work the cash register, stock shelves, and perform other clerical duties. They can also work in hospitals and nursing homes, helping to deliver and dispense medicine. They do most of their work standing, and they may work nights and weekends, since many pharmacies are open 24 hours a day.

Subjects to Study

Math, computer skills, chemistry, biology, health, English

Discover More

Visit your local pharmacy and ask the pharmacist if you can "apprentice." He or she might let you help out with stocking or cleaning shelves. While you work, watch the pharmacist on the job and ask about training opportunities in your area.

Education & Training
Moderate-term OJT

Earnings
$$

Related Jobs

Pharmacists, pharmacy aides, dental assistants, licensed practical and licensed vocational nurses, medical transcriptionists, medical records and health information technicians, occupational therapist assistants and aides, physical therapist assistants and aides, surgical technologists

Job Outlook
Rapid increase

Radiologic Technologists & Technicians

On the Job

Radiologic technologists and technicians work in hospitals and clinics. They operate the machines that take X-ray pictures or magnetic resolution pictures of people's bones and internal organs. They must wear badges that measure the amount of radiation they are exposed to on the job. These workers might work nights or weekends and might be on call during odd hours. They are on their feet most of the day and must be strong enough to lift patients.

SOMETHING EXTRA

The first X ray ever taken was by a German scientist named Conrad Roentgen, who discovered them quite by accident. He called them X rays (rather than Roentgen rays as his colleagues suggested) because the type of radiation was unknown. The first X ray of the human body was actually a picture of his wife's hand, ring and all.

Subjects to Study

Biology, chemistry, physics, math, computer science

Discover More

You can get more information about this job by writing to the American Society of Radiologic Technologists, 15000 Central Ave. S.E., Albuquerque, NM 87123-3917, or visit their Web site at www.asrt.org.

Related Jobs

Cardiovascular technologists and technicians, clinical laboratory technologists and technicians, diagnostic medical sonographers, nuclear medicine technologists, respiratory therapists

Education & Training
Associate degree

Earnings
$$$$

Job Outlook
Above-average increase

Surgical Technologists

On the Job

Surgical technologists set up equipment in the operating room, prepare patients for surgery, and take patients to and from the operating room. They help the surgical team "scrub" and put on gloves, masks, and surgical clothing. During an operation, they help with supplies and instruments and operate lights and equipment. After the operation, they restock the operating room. Surgical technicians must be able to stay calm and steady in stressful circumstances.

Subjects to Study

Health, biology, chemistry, math, anatomy, English, foreign languages

Discover More

Surgical technicians must be comfortable dealing with operations of all kinds. One way to test your tolerance for this is to take a biology course in which you dissect an animal. Another way is to watch informational television programs where actual surgeries are performed.

Related Jobs

Dental assistants, licensed practical and licensed vocational nurses, clinical laboratory technologists and technicians, medical assistants

Education & Training
Voc/tech training

Earnings
$$$$

Job Outlook
Rapid increase

Veterinary Technologists and Technicians

On the Job

Veterinary technologists and technicians perform many of the same duties for a veterinarian that a nurse would for a physician, including handling laboratory and clinical work such as urine and blood tests. They may work in private vets' offices, zoos, research facilities, and other places where veterinarians work. Some of the work can be unpleasant and even dangerous.

SOMETHING EXTRA

Veterinary technologists and technicians often have to help put sick animals to sleep. It's difficult for them emotionally, but they know that it's usually the kindest thing you can do for an animal that is in pain. It's quick, and the only pain for the animal is the stick with the needle. They also often have to help the pet's owners to feel better on this difficult day.

Subjects to Study

Biology, math, chemistry, zoology, communication skills

Discover More

Volunteer to help out at your local Humane Society or vet's office. Watch the veterinary technicians at work and see the kinds of things they do to help the vet and the animals. It's often unpleasant work, but you do get to be around animals!

Related Jobs

Animal care and service workers, veterinarians

Education & Training
Associate degree

Earnings
$$

Job Outlook
Rapid increase

Service Occupations

Dental Assistants

Centuries ago people believed that tooth decay was caused by worms in the gums. The only way to remove the decay was to pull the tooth. This was a painful process, because they had no anesthesia to numb the area first. Often, the dentist's assistant had the job of holding the patient down while the dentist yanked out the tooth. Today, dental assistants spend time calming patients' fears instead of pinning them down.

On the Job

Dental assistants help dentists during patient exams and treatments. They schedule appointments, keep patient records, handle billing, and order supplies. Those with lab duties clean removable dentures and make temporary crowns for teeth. They wear gloves and masks to protect themselves from diseases and germs. Many work evenings and Saturdays, and they spend a good part of their time on their feet.

Subjects to Study

Biology, chemistry, health, business courses, math, computer skills, psychology

Discover More

Visit your dentist's office and ask about careers in this field. Does your dentist employ an assistant? What does he or she do? Ask the assistant about training and the job.

Related Jobs

Medical assistants, occupational therapist assistants and aides, pharmacy aides, pharmacy technicians, physical therapist assistants and aides

Education & Training
Moderate-term OJT

Earnings
$$$

Job Outlook
Rapid increase

Massage Therapists

On the Job

These therapists use massage to treat muscle pain, relieve stress, rehabilitate sport injuries, and promote general health. Massage therapists can specialize in 80 different types of massage. Some work in hospitals, nursing homes, or sports facilities, though a good number operate out of private offices or travel to homes and businesses. Massage therapy is physically demanding work and requires therapists to be on their feet most of the day.

Subjects to Study

English, psychology, physical education, anatomy, business courses

Discover More

The best way to learn more about massage therapy is to practice it. Start by giving shoulder rubs, as that is often a source of muscular tension. Be sure to try out a variety of motions. Also visit your local library for guides on how to give a proper massage.

Related Jobs

Physical therapists, physical therapist assistants and aides, chiropractors

Education & Training
Voc/tech training

Earnings
$$$$

Job Outlook
Above-average increase

Medical Assistants

On the Job

Medical assistants help keep your doctor's office running smoothly. They answer phones, greet patients, schedule appointments, arrange for hospital admissions and tests, handle billing, and file records. They may take medical histories, explain treatments to patients, and help doctors with exams. They also may prepare and perform laboratory tests. They must have good people skills. Many work evenings and weekends.

Subjects to Study

Math, health, biology, computer skills, office skills, English, foreign languages

Discover More

Ask your own doctor if you can spend a day in the office watching what the medical assistants do. Maybe you can help file papers, answer phones, or make copies.

Related Jobs

Dental assistants, medical records and health information technicians, occupational therapist assistants and aides, pharmacy aides, physical therapist assistants and aides

Education & Training
Moderate-term OJT

Earnings
$$

Job Outlook
Rapid increase

Medical Transcriptionists

On the Job

Medical transcriptionists listen to dictated recordings made by doctors and transcribe them into medical reports, letters, and other written materials. They use a special headset, using a foot pedal to pause the tape when necessary, and type the materials into a computer, editing it for grammar and clarity. Some transcriptionists work in doctor's offices or hospitals, but many work as freelancers from home.

SOMETHING EXTRA

Why would anyone need a written version of what a doctor says during surgery? In long, complex operations, surgeons often talk into a tape recorder, describing what they are doing and finding. Those tapes are then transcribed and filed. If a complication arises later, the doctor can simply go back to the files and double-check his or her work, looking for clues to the complication.

Subjects to Study

Computer skills, English, anatomy, biology, foreign languages

Discover More

Make a recording of yourself or a friend reading material out loud from a book or magazine. Then try typing the material from the recording without making any mistakes. Even if the person on the recording reads slowly, you'll have to type fast to keep up!

Related Jobs

Court reporters; human resources assistants, except payroll and timekeeping; receptionists and information clerks; secretaries and administrative assistants; medical assistants; medical records and health information technicians

Education & Training
Voc/tech training

Earnings
$$$

Job Outlook
Above-average increase

Nursing, Psychiatric & Home Health Aides

On the Job

Nursing and psychiatric aides care for patients in hospitals, nursing homes, and mental health clinics. Home health aides care for patients in the home. All of these workers feed, bathe, and dress patients, help them get in and out of bed, take temperatures and blood pressures, and set up equipment. They report any signs or changes to doctors or nurses. Most work some weekends and evening hours. They must be strong enough to lift and move patients.

Subjects to Study

Health, nutrition, anatomy, communication skills, English, psychology

Discover More

Volunteer at a nursing home in your community. You might be asked to read to patients, make deliveries, help with activities, or just visit with a patient who is lonely.

Related Jobs

Childcare workers, licensed practical and licensed vocational nurses, medical assistants, occupational therapist assistants and aides, personal and home care aides, physical therapist assistants and aides, registered nurses

Education & Training
Short-term OJT

Earnings
$$

Job Outlook
Rapid increase

Occupational Therapist Assistants & Aides

On the Job

Occupational therapist assistants help therapists in clinics, rehab centers, nursing homes, and home health care programs. They help injured patients regain use of damaged muscles. They might help patients learn to use wheelchairs or other devices. They also help mentally disabled patients learn living skills like cooking and keeping a checkbook. Occupational therapy aides keep patient records and set up equipment. These workers must be strong enough to lift and move patients and equipment.

SOMETHING EXTRA

Some people enjoy the 9-to-5 routine. But for many, spending eight hours a day behind a desk would be torture. Occupational therapist assistants who work with mentally disabled adults may travel to several homes and facilities each day, taking clients grocery shopping, teaching them cooking skills, helping them apply for assistance, or driving them on errands.

Subjects to Study

Psychology, anatomy, physical education, communication skills, English, health

Discover More

Try teaching younger children an outdoor activity or game. Plan out the activity, decide whether it's appropriate for their age group, then teach the children how to play. Watch to make sure they play fairly and safely.

Related Jobs

Occupational therapists, dental assistants, medical assistants, pharmacy aides, pharmacy technicians, physical therapist assistants and aides

Education & Training
Short-term OJT to Associate degree

Earnings
$$$$

Job Outlook
Rapid increase

Pharmacy Aides

On the Job

Pharmacy aides help licensed pharmacists by answering phones, stocking shelves, and running the cash register. They also maintain patient files, prepare insurance papers, and take inventory of medicines and supplies. Some also clean pharmacy equipment. They may work evenings or weekends; some even work overnight shifts in 24- hour pharmacies.

Subjects to Study

English, foreign languages, biology, chemistry, computer skills, business courses

Discover More

Talk with the pharmacist at your local drug store. What opportunities are available for students wanting to work part-time? Maybe you'll land a job!

Education & Training
Short-term OJT

Related Jobs

Pharmacy technicians, cashiers, stock clerks and order fillers, dental assistants, licensed practical and licensed vocational nurses, medical transcriptionists, medical records and health information technicians, occupational therapist assistants and aides, physical therapist assistants and aides, surgical technologists

Earnings
$

Job Outlook
Average increase

Physical Therapist Assistants & Aides

On the Job

Physical therapist assistants help physical therapists care for patients in hospitals, nursing homes, and home health care programs. They help patients recovering from injuries or disease improve their mobility, relieve pain, and regain muscle use. They may help with exercises, give massages, and apply hot/cold packs. Physical therapy aides keep equipment in good order, move patients to and from the treatment area, and help with record keeping.

> ### SOMETHING EXTRA
>
> When LeBron James pulls a muscle, who does he turn to for help? A sports medicine specialist is a physical therapist specializing in sports-related injuries. These workers help athletes prepare their bodies for competition, and they are on hand during sporting events to help in emergencies. After an injury or illness, they work with an athlete to help him or her rebuild muscle tone and agility. Of course with LeBron's salary, he could probably hire the Surgeon General.

Subjects to Study

Health, anatomy, physical education, communication skills, psychology

Discover More

Ask your gym teacher to show you some exercises you can use to strengthen your own muscles. Then teach these exercises to family members or friends. Set up a regular exercise schedule for yourself.

Related Jobs

Physical therapists, dental assistants, medical assistants, occupational therapist assistants and aides, pharmacy aides, pharmacy technicians

Education & Training
Short-term OJT to Associate degree

Earnings
$$$$

Job Outlook
Rapid increase

Correctional Officers

On the Job

Correctional officers guard people who are awaiting trial and those who have been convicted of crimes. They keep order and enforce rules in jails or prisons and assign and supervise inmates' work. They help inmates with personal problems and report any bad behavior. To prevent escapes, they stand guard in towers and at gates. They work indoors and outdoors under very stressful and potentially dangerous conditions. Many work nights and weekends. These workers must be strong and able to use firearms.

Subjects to Study

Physical education, driver's education, psychology, sociology

Education & Training
Moderate-term OJT to Work experience

Discover More

Some state prisons give tours to the public or to school groups. Check to see whether you can visit one to learn more about this job.

Earnings
$$$$

Related Jobs

Security guards and gaming surveillance officers, police and detectives, probation officers and correctional treatment specialists

Job Outlook
Little change

Firefighting Occupations

On the Job

Firefighters protect people from the dangers of fires. They must stay physically fit and strong. At the scene of a fire, they rescue victims, perform emergency medical aid, and operate and maintain equipment. During their shifts, firefighters live at the fire station. Most work 50 hours a week or more. Forest firefighters may parachute into a fire area to put out fires and dig a fire line. Firefighting is one of the most dangerous jobs in the U.S. economy.

SOMETHING EXTRA

Firefighters who battle wildfires are a special breed. During the hot, dry months of late summer, they travel from state to state, helping local firefighters battle forest fires. They may jump from air planes into a fire zone to dig fire lines. If a fire travels too quickly and they get trapped, they drop to the ground and cover themselves with a special fireproofed tent. They wait until the fire has passed over them, get up, and keep on fighting the flames. It's one of the hottest jobs on the market.

Subjects to Study

Physical science, chemistry, driver's education, physical education

Discover More

Tour the fire station in your neighborhood. Ask the firefighters about their jobs, the training they receive, and the risks of the job. Then ask them if you can slide down the pole.

Related Jobs

Emergency medical technicians and paramedics, police and detectives

Education & Training
Moderate-term OJT to Bachelor's degree

Earnings
$$$$

Job Outlook
Above-average increase

Police & Detectives

On the Job

Police, detectives, and special agents protect people from crime and violence. They patrol highways, issue traffic tickets, and help accident victims. They also collect evidence and investigate crimes. Police detectives often testify in court about their cases. Most work some evenings and weekends. Police work is dangerous and stressful.

Subjects to Study

English, psychology, sociology, chemistry, physics, driver's education, physical education, foreign languages

Discover More

Police officers often check for fingerprints at the scene of a crime. Make your own fingerprinting kit with talcum powder, a paintbrush, and a magnifying glass. Dust the powder lightly on a solid, shiny surface such as a doorknob. Blow gently. The powder will blow away, except where the greasy marks are. Brush the powdered spots lightly with the paintbrush and examine the prints with the glass.

Education & Training
Long-term OJT to Work experience

Earnings
$$$$

Job Outlook
Average increase

Related Jobs

Correctional officers, private detectives and investigators, security guards and gaming surveillance officers

Private Detectives & Investigators

On the Job

Private detectives and investigators work for lawyers, insurance companies, and other kinds of businesses. They gather information for trials, track down people who owe companies money, and conduct background checks. Some are self-employed and specialize in searching for missing persons or finding information for divorce cases. They may spend long hours watching a person or place, hunting for clues, and interviewing people. They often work irregular hours and travel, and the work may be dangerous.

SOMETHING EXTRA

Say "private detective" and many people think of macho movie detectives in trench coats with cigarettes dangling from their lips. But did you know that many detectives these days are women? A detective's greatest asset is an ability to blend into the background, so detective agencies often use women to investigate other women. These female sleuths can follow suspects into gyms, shopping malls, and even restrooms without calling attention to themselves.

Subjects to Study

English, psychology, sociology, chemistry, physics, driver's education, physical education, foreign languages

Discover More

An investigator's main job is collecting information. Use your investigative skills to find interesting information about this job. What can you find at the library or on the Internet that you didn't know before?

Related Jobs

Bill and account collectors; claims adjusters, appraisers, examiners, and investigators; police and detectives; security guards and gaming surveillance officers; accountants and auditors; financial analysts and personal finance advisors

Education & Training
Work experience

Earnings
$$$$

Job Outlook
Above-average increase

Security Guards & Gaming Surveillance Officers

On the Job

Guards protect property from fire, theft, vandalism, and break-ins. They patrol the area, usually on foot, or check people entering and leaving the area. Guards may carry a nightstick or gun. Most work some nights and weekends, and the work can be dangerous. Gaming surveillance officers work in casinos and gaming parlors, watching for people who are trying to cheat the system.

Subjects to Study

English, driver's education, psychology, physical education, communication skills, computer skills

Education & Training

Short-term OJT to Work experience

Earnings

$$

Job Outlook

Average increase

Discover More

Call a security company in your area and ask if you can speak with someone who hires security guards. Ask that person about the skills you would need to be a guard. Does the company provide training?

Related Jobs

Correctional officers, police and detectives, private detectives and investigators

Chefs, Cooks & Food Preparation Workers

On the Job

Chefs and cooks plan and make meals in restaurants, schools, cafeterias, and hospitals. They supervise other workers, order supplies, and plan menus. Kitchen workers help chefs and cooks by chopping vegetables, measuring ingredients, and stirring soups and sauces. They also keep the kitchen clean and wash dishes. These workers are on their feet all day in crowded, hot kitchens. Most work evenings and weekends, and many work part-time.

SOMETHING EXTRA

Did you know that not all chefs work in restaurants? Some work for airlines and cruise ships, planning menus for on-board meals. Some are self-employed, operating their own catering companies. Many celebrities—from Oprah Winfrey to Mick Jagger—employ private chefs to cook for them. But the most prestigious cooking group might be those who prepare meals for kings and queens, prime ministers, and presidents. These elite chefs even have their own club!

Subjects to Study

Family and consumer sciences, nutrition, math, health

Discover More

Cook a three-course meal for your family. Ask a parent to help you look through some cookbooks or look for recipes online. Be sure to pick an appetizer, a main course, and a dessert. Of course you may need some help from other members of the family to put it all together.

Related Jobs

Food processing occupations, food service managers, food and beverage serving and related workers

Education & Training
Short-term OJT to Work experience

Earnings
$

Job Outlook
Average increase

Food & Beverage Serving & Related Workers

On the Job

Food and beverage service workers deal with customers in restaurants. They take food orders, fill drink orders, serve food, prepare the bill, and may accept payment. Other workers clean dirty tables and reset them with silverware and napkins. These workers spend hours on their feet. They carry heavy trays and must serve customers quickly and courteously. Most work evenings and weekends, and many work part-time.

Subjects to Study

English, foreign languages, math, speech, family and consumer sciences

Education & Training
Short-term OJT

Earnings
$

Job Outlook
Average increase

Discover More

The best way to learn about the restaurant industry is to work in it. Look for a part-time job at a fast-food restaurant. Or talk to friends who have worked in one. Find out what they liked and disliked about the job. What hours and days did they work? How much did they make in tips, if any?

Related Jobs

Flight attendants, gaming services occupations, retail salespersons

Building Cleaning Workers

On the Job

Building cleaning workers keep offices, schools, hospitals, hotels, and other public buildings clean and in good condition. They clean, repair, empty trash cans, paint, and mow lawns. Cleaning supervisors assign jobs, supervise workers, and order supplies. These people often work evenings and weekends. The work can be dirty and strenuous.

SOMETHING EXTRA

What would you do if you found a diamond ring under a pillow? Or a suitcase full of cash in a closet? Or a small child in the bathroom? If you're a hotel housekeeper, you might just shrug your shoulders and call the front desk. These workers routinely find expensive, unusual, and downright bizarre things in the rooms they clean. People in a hurry to pack up and get on the road are apt to leave behind anything—even their child!

Subjects to Study

Shop courses, family and consumer sciences, physical education

Discover More

Talk to the janitor at your school. Make a list of all the chores and different tasks he or she does. What is the best part of the job? What is the worst part of the job?

Related Jobs

Pest control workers, general maintenance and repair workers, grounds maintenance workers

Education & Training
Short-term OJT to Work experience

Earnings
$

Job Outlook
Average increase

Grounds Maintenance Workers

On the Job

Grounds maintenance workers care for lawns, trees, gardens, and other plants and keep the grounds free of litter. They may prune, feed, and water gardens and mow and water lawns at private homes and public places. They also maintain athletic fields, golf courses, cemeteries, and parks. They work outside in all kinds of weather. Many are self-employed and work seasonally.

Subjects to Study

Biology, zoology, botany, driver's education, business math

Discover More

Plant some flowers around your home or in a pot inside. Start with some easy annuals like snapdragons, petunias, or marigolds. Next, try something trickier, like orchids or roses. Can you make your flowers grow?

Related Jobs

Agricultural workers; farmers, ranchers, and agricultural managers; forest, conservation, and logging workers; landscape architects; biological scientists

Education & Training
Short-term OJT to Work experience

Earnings
$$

Job Outlook
Above-average increase

Pest Control Workers

On the Job

Pest control workers find and kill roaches, rats, mice, spiders, termites, ants, bees—all kinds of pests that invade people's homes and offices. They use chemicals, poisonous fumes, traps, and electrical equipment to eliminate pests. They travel to homes and offices to perform their work, often crawling and climbing into tight places. They wear protective gear, including respirators, gloves, and goggles. Some work evenings and weekends.

Subjects to Study

Biology, chemistry, zoology, physical education, computer skills, math

Discover More

Learn more about the kinds of bugs that inhabit your state by starting a bug collection. Find as many different kinds of insects as possible, then mount them on heavy-duty white cardboard using straight pins. Identify them using a field guide from the library, then label each specimen you find and learn about its habitat, food, and natural prey.

Related Jobs

Building cleaning workers; grounds maintenance workers; carpenters; electricians; heating, air-conditioning, and refrigeration mechanics and installers

Education & Training
Moderate-term OJT

Earnings
$$$

Job Outlook
Above-average increase

Animal Care & Service Workers

On the Job

Animal care and service workers feed, water, bathe, and exercise animals in clinics, kennels, and zoos. They play with the animals, watch them for illness or injury, and clean and repair their cages. Kennel staff care for cats and dogs; stable workers groom, exercise, and care for horses; and zookeepers care for wild and exotic animals. They may work outdoors in all kinds of weather. The work can be dirty and dangerous. Many work weekends and nights, and some travel with animals to sports events or shows.

Subjects to Study

Life sciences, zoology, biology, chemistry, physical education

Education & Training

Short-term OJT to Moderate-term OJT

Earnings

$

Job Outlook

Above-average increase

Discover More

You can learn more about this occupation by volunteering at a zoo or animal shelter. You might play with or cuddle small animals, clean cages, put out food and water, or take animals for walks.

Related Jobs

Farmers, ranchers, and agricultural managers; agricultural workers; veterinarians; veterinary technologists and technicians; veterinary assistants; biological scientists; medical scientists

Barbers, Cosmetologists & Other Personal Appearance Workers

On the Job

These workers help people look their best. They cut, shampoo, style, color, and perm hair. They may fit customers for hairpieces, shave male customers, and give facial massages and advice on makeup. Many cosmetologists are trained to give manicures. They also keep customer records and order supplies. These workers spend a lot of time on their feet. Many work part time, and many are self-employed.

SOMETHING EXTRA

In Hollywood's "beauty wars," any small advantage can mean the difference between getting a role and going broke. That's why actors and actresses change their hairstyles, their wardrobes, and their looks so often. Hairstylists in Tinseltown must stay current with the latest styles and trends. A stylist who caters to the newest stars' whims can become almost as well known and wealthy as the stars themselves.

Subjects to Study

Communication skills, business courses, accounting, speech, health

Discover More

Set up a beauty salon at home and practice on yourself or a friend. Look through magazines for the latest styles, then wash and style your friend's hair.

Related Jobs

Massage therapists, fitness workers

Education & Training
Short-term OJT to Voc/tech training

Earnings
$$

Job Outlook
Average increase

Childcare Workers

Have you ever walked into a day-care center? Often, the scene looks like barely controlled chaos. Young children don't sit at desks and read or color quietly. They shout, dance, cartwheel, run, and sing out loud. That's how they learn. It takes a special kind of person to work with children this age. Childcare workers must be creative, patient, and calm, and have a healthy sense of humor!

On the Job

Childcare workers care for children under the age of five. Those caring for infants and toddlers may change diapers, heat bottles, and rock children to sleep. Those caring for preschoolers serve meals, play games, read stories, and organize activities to help the children socialize and learn new skills. A third of these workers actually run childcare services out of their homes. The work can be tiring, and workers must be strong enough to lift and move children.

Subjects to Study

English, child development, psychology, family and consumer sciences, art, music, drama, health, speech

Education & Training

Short-term OJT

Earnings

$

Job Outlook

Average increase

Discover More

The easiest way to learn about this job is to baby-sit or help someone else take care of young children. It's also a good way to pick up a couple of bucks.

Related Jobs

Teacher assistants; teachers—preschool, kindergarten, elementary, middle, and secondary; teachers—special education

Fitness Workers

On the Job

Fitness workers help people work out and get healthy. They teach proper exercise methods and lead exercise groups. Personal trainers work one-on-one with individuals to help them reach their fitness goals. Group exercise instructors, on the other hand, lead sessions of a particular activity like yoga or aerobics. Naturally these workers must be in good shape, though they are still prone to injury.

SOMETHING EXTRA

How much exercise is enough? Scientists, doctors, and researchers have debated this and the answers vary. But nearly all agree that a half an hour of moderate physical activity a day is enough to keep your heart healthy and your energy up. Have you had your half hour of exercise yet today?

Subjects to Study

Physical education, biology, chemistry, psychology, dance

Discover More

Plan a weekly exercise routine for you and your family, making sure you to get some kind of exercise each day of the week. This could include both indoor and outdoor activities, from doing an aerobics video workout to riding bikes to just taking a walk. See whether you notice a difference in your energy and appearance after a few weeks of this routine.

Related Jobs

Athletes, coaches, umpires, and related workers

Education & Training
Voc/tech training

Earnings
$$$

Job Outlook
Rapid increase

Flight Attendants

On the Job

Flight attendants help keep airline passengers safe and comfortable. In an emergency, they help passengers react calmly and quickly. They also stock the plane with food, drinks, blankets, first-aid kits, and other supplies. During the flight, they serve food and drinks and answer questions. They may administer first aid to passengers who become ill. They work irregular hours, travel extensively, stay on their feet, and must remain calm in emergencies.

Subjects to Study

English, communication skills, foreign languages, speech, first aid, health, physical education

Discover More

For more information on becoming a flight attendant, visit the Web site for the Association of Flight Attendants: www.afanet.org.

Related Jobs

Emergency medical technicians and paramedics, firefighting occupations

Education & Training
Long-term OJT

Earnings
$$$$

Job Outlook
Average increase

Gaming Services Occupations

On the Job

Most gaming services workers are employed by casinos— places where people play games of chance for money. Supervisors oversee the gaming tables and workers. Slot attendants watch over the slot machines, making sure everything is working smoothly. Gaming dealers operate games such as blackjack, craps, and roulette. All gaming workers must be licensed and have good customer-relations skills.

Subjects to Study

English, foreign languages, math, business courses, psychology

Discover More

You can learn the rules for different card and table games used in casinos, and about casino careers, by checking out www.americangaming.org. Or ask a parent or friend to teach you how to play.

Related Jobs

Security guards and gaming surveillance officers, sales worker supervisors, cashiers, retail salespersons, gaming cage workers, tellers

Education & Training
Work experience to Voc/tech training

Earnings
$$

Job Outlook
Above-average increase

Personal & Home Care Aides

On the Job

Home health and personal care aides help elderly, disabled, and seriously ill patients to live at home instead of in a nursing home. They clean, do laundry, prepare meals, and help with personal hygiene. They also check the patient's pulse and blood pressure and give medication. Aides keep records of each patient's condition and progress. They often work part-time and weekend hours.

Subjects to Study

Family and consumer sciences, nutrition, health, first aid, English, foreign languages

Discover More

Set up your own "rent-a-kid" service in your neighborhood. Can you help out in your neighbors' homes by cleaning, ironing clothes, running errands, or doing yard work to earn extra money?

Related Jobs

Childcare workers; nursing, psychiatric, and home health aides; occupational therapist assistants and aides; physical therapist assistants and aides; social and human services assistants

Education & Training
Short-term OJT

Earnings
$

Job Outlook
Rapid increase

Recreation Workers

On the Job

Recreation workers often work as camp counselors or coaches, organizing leisure activities at parks, health clubs, camps, tourist sites, and other places. They teach people how to use recreation equipment properly and safely. They often work nights and weekends. Recreation workers may work in state and national parks, health clubs, or even on cruise ships. Many work part time.

SOMETHING EXTRA

People from all walks of life can get a taste of the wilderness with Outward Bound expeditions. Teenagers, senior citizens, school groups, and business groups can take two-week treks into the mountains. There, they go hiking, white-water rafting, rock climbing, and backcountry skiing. Outward Bound trainers help the adventurers build their self-confidence and their teamwork, while making sure they are safe.

Subjects to Study

English, communication skills, business courses, accounting, physical education, swimming, art, music, drama, sports

Discover More

Call your local YMCA, YWCA, Boys' or Girls' Club, or community center and volunteer to help out. You might be asked to watch younger children, teach them games, or help maintain equipment.

Related Jobs

Counselors, probation officers and correctional treatment specialists, psychologists, recreational therapists, social workers

Education & Training
Bachelor's degree

Earnings
$$

Job Outlook
Average increase

Sales & Related Occupations

Advertising Sales Agents

On the Job

Advertising sales agents do exactly what the name suggests—they sell advertising, including space in publications, signs and billboards, and television and radio time. Some work with businesses to decide what forms of advertising will work best. Others work for media companies to sell the space they have for advertising. The work can be stressful due to irregular hours and sales quotas.

Subjects to Study

Math, English, communication skills, computer skills, business courses, art, journalism, economics

Discover More

If your school has a newspaper, find out how you can get involved in its production. Contact local businesses around your school like grocery stores and restaurants to see if they would be willing to buy advertising space in your school paper. Or simply see if they would be willing to sponsor a charity fund drive, and then plan one with your class.

Education & Training
Moderate-term OJT

Earnings
$$$$

Job Outlook
Average increase

Related Jobs

Advertising, marketing, promotions, public relations, and sales managers; insurance sales agents; real estate brokers and sales agents; sales engineers; sales representatives, wholesale and manufacturing; securities, commodities, and financial services sales agents

Cashiers

On the Job

Cashiers add up customers' bills, take their money, and give change. They also fill out charge forms for credit cards and give receipts. Cashiers are responsible for the money they collect during their shifts. They cannot leave their cash drawers without permission from their supervisor. Cashiers use cash registers, scanners, and computers regularly.

SOMETHING EXTRA

A cashier receives a specific amount of money in a cash drawer at the beginning of each work shift. The cashier counts this "bank" of money, for which he or she is responsible. At the end of the shift the cashier counts the bank again and compares the total to the sales information. Most employers understand if the drawer comes up short occasionally, but repeated shortages can get you fired.

Subjects to Study

Math, English, communication skills, computer skills, business courses

Discover More

Volunteer to work as a cashier at a church, club, or family rummage sale. Make sure you have enough money in the cash drawer to make change for the customers. Save the tags from the items paid for at your cash drawer. Add the total sales to the amount that was in your cash drawer before the sale. Then count the money in your drawer. Does it balance?

Related Jobs

Tellers, counter and rental clerks, food and beverage serving and related workers, gaming cage workers, postal service workers, retail salespersons

Education & Training
Short-term OJT

Earnings
$

Job Outlook
Little change

Counter & Rental Clerks

SOMETHING EXTRA

If you plan to go to a formal dance at your school, you will probably deal with a rental clerk. Rental clerks at formal-wear companies help many students rent their tuxedos, gowns, and accessories for the big night. Some students even rent a limousine for the occasion. In fact, the average cost for a couple to go to prom nowadays is nearly a thousand dollars. You might start saving now.

On the Job

Counter and rental clerks take orders, figure out fees, receive payment, and accept returns. They answer questions about what kinds of items are in stock and how much they cost. They must know about the company's products, services, and policies. Some fill out forms and tickets by hand, but most use computers and scanners. They generally spend long periods of time on their feet.

Subjects to Study

Math, English, communication skills, computer skills, business courses

Discover More

Go to a video store and rent a video or DVD. Watch what the rental clerk does to rent the item to you and to make sure that you will return it. If the store isn't busy, stop and ask questions about the job.

Related Jobs

Tellers, cashiers, food and beverage serving and related workers, gaming cage workers, postal service workers, retail salespersons

Education & Training
Short-term OJT

Earnings
$

Job Outlook
Above-average increase

Demonstrators, Product Promoters & Models

On the Job

Demonstrators show products to customers, either in retail stores or in private homes. Product promoters try to convince stores to carry new products. They may set up displays in stores or host special activities to show off their products. Models pose for photographs to display clothing, makeup, and other accessories. They also wear designer clothes during fashion shows and work in television commercials. All of these workers travel as part of their jobs.

SOMETHING EXTRA

Nearly everyone recognizes Kate Moss and Tyra Banks, but how about Ellen Sirot? Well, you might not recognize her name or face, but you might just recognize her hands. They've been photographed holding everything from soft drinks to cell phones. She's a hand model, and she makes a living showing off her slim wrists, tapering fingers, and healthy nails. If your hands aren't your best feature, how about something else? The modeling industry uses foot models, leg models, hair models, and even lip models. Your face may not be in Vogue, but your earlobes might!

Subjects to Study

Communication skills, marketing, math, photography, speech, sociology, foreign languages

Discover More

Do a product demonstration for your class. Design a catchy poster and slogan, write a script, and come up with a gimmick to draw people's attention. Try to convince your classmates that your product is one they definitely want to have.

Related Jobs

Actors, producers, and directors; insurance sales agents; real estate brokers and sales agents; retail salespersons; sales representatives, wholesale and manufacturing

Education & Training
Moderate-term OJT

Earnings
$$

Job Outlook
Average increase

Insurance Sales Agents

People buy insurance to protect their assets. But not all assets are cars or houses. The famous insurance group Lloyd's of London has issued some odd insurance policies in recent years. Some of these policies include accident insurance for Russian cosmonauts traveling to the MIR space station; coverage in case of a crocodile attack; and insuring a famous model's legs, a singer's vocal chords, and a food critic's taste buds.

On the Job

Insurance agents sell insurance policies to people and businesses. Insurance policies protect the people and companies who buy them against different kinds of losses. Common policies include health, life, and car insurance. Insurance agents and brokers help people choose the policies that best meet their needs. Agents work for a single insurance company. Insurance brokers are independent and sell insurance for several different companies.

Subjects to Study

Math, accounting, economics, government, psychology, sociology, speech, computer skills

Education & Training
Bachelor's degree

Discover More

Ask your parents what kinds of insurance they have. How did they choose their insurance plans? Do they receive insurance through their employers?

Earnings
$$$$

Related Jobs

Real estate brokers and sales agents; securities, commodities, and financial services sales agents; financial analysts and personal financial advisors; financial managers; insurance underwriters; claims adjusters, appraisers, examiners, and investigators

Job Outlook
Little change

Real Estate Brokers & Sales Agents

On the Job

Real estate agents and brokers help people buy and sell homes and rental properties. Real estate agents show homes, help buyers get financing, and make sure the contract conditions are met. Brokers may sell houses and rent and manage properties. These workers must know and understand their local housing market. They also must have a real estate license.

Subjects to Study

Math, English, accounting, economics, business courses, communication skills, computer skills, psychology

Discover More

You can usually find free real estate and rental magazines at grocery stores or drugstores. Look through one to find out what homes and properties are available in your community. How much do homes and apartments in your area cost? Then flip through and see if you can find your dream house. How much does *it* cost?

Related Jobs

Insurance sales agents; retail salespersons; sales representatives, wholesale and manufacturing; securities, commodities, and financial services sales agents; property, real estate, and community association managers

Education & Training
Work experience to Voc/tech training

Earnings
$$$$

Job Outlook
Average increase

Retail Salespersons

On the Job

Retail salespersons help customers choose and buy all kinds of items, from sweaters and makeup to lumber and plumbing. Their primary job is to interest customers in whatever products they are selling. They also fill out sales checks, take payment, bag purchases, and give change and receipts. Most sales workers are responsible for keeping track of the money in their cash registers.

Subjects to Study

Math, English, communication skills, computer skills, psychology

Discover More

Watch the sales workers the next time you go shopping. What jobs do they do? How do they approach customers? How do they help you? Does their mood or approach affect your desire to buy their products?

Related Jobs

Sales representatives, wholesale and manufacturing; securities, commodities, and financial services sales agents; counter and rental clerks; real estate brokers and sales agents; purchasing managers, buyers, and purchasing agents; insurance sales agents; sales engineers; cashiers

Education & Training
Short-term OJT

Earnings
$

Job Outlook
Average increase

Sales Engineers

On the Job

Sales engineers work for companies that produce complex products—such as chemicals or technical tools. They help customers decide which products or services will work best for them. Selling is an important part of the job, but sales engineers also help their customers learn to use the products they buy. They also may help companies produce better materials based on customer feedback.

SOMETHING EXTRA

We've all heard the jokes about traveling salesmen. Sales engineers are a far cry from the people peddling vacuum cleaners and encyclopedias door-to-door. Their customers are large and small businesses that need specialized services and products—everything from production machinery to dry-cleaning chemicals, and from huge database systems to tiny electrical components. They don't go door-to-door, but they do travel a lot. Some spend months at a time on the road, racking up frequent-flyer miles!

Subjects to Study

Math, chemistry, biology, physics, English, foreign languages, psychology

Discover More

For more information on becoming a sales engineer, contact the Manufacturers' Agents National Association at www.manaonline.org, or the Manufacturers Representatives Educational Research Foundation at www.mrerf.org.

Related Jobs

Advertising, marketing, promotions, public relations, and sales managers; engineers; insurance sales agents; purchasing managers, buyers, and purchasing agents; real estate brokers and sales agents; sales representatives, wholesale and manufacturing; securities, commodities, and financial services sales agents

Education & Training
Bachelor's degree

Earnings
$$$$$

Job Outlook
Average increase

Sales Representatives, Wholesale & Manufacturing

SOMETHING EXTRA

Most sales representatives are paid on commission. Instead of receiving a regular paycheck, they get paid based on their sales: The more they sell, the more money they make. Few or no sales means little or no money. Many sales means big paychecks. Salespeople must learn to budget and pay their bills knowing that their income is unpredictable.

On the Job

Manufacturing and wholesale sales representatives sell products to businesses, government agencies, and other institutions, often traveling for several days or weeks at a time. They answer questions about their products and show clients how the products can meet their needs and save them money. They also take orders and resolve problems or complaints about their merchandise.

Subjects to Study

Math, English, speech, communication skills, accounting, business courses, psychology, foreign languages, computer skills

Discover More

Think of some businesses in your community (such as hospitals, grocery stores, and restaurants) that might order products from manufacturers' sales representatives. What kind of products would each of these businesses buy?

Education & Training
Moderate-term OJT

Earnings
$$$$

Job Outlook
Average increase

Related Jobs

Advertising, marketing, promotions, public relations, and sales managers; insurance sales agents; purchasing managers, buyers, and purchasing agents; real estate brokers and sales agents; retail salespersons; sales engineers; securities, commodities, and financial services sales agents

Sales Worker Supervisors

On the Job

Sales worker supervisors work in all kinds of stores—dress shops, toy stores, convenience stores, and bakeries to name a few. They hire, train, and supervise workers. They also make the schedule of who will work what hours. They order supplies, keep the books, make bank deposits, and often wait on customers. Most work evenings and weekends, and they spend a lot of time on their feet.

SOMETHING EXTRA

Many people in our economy work standard work-week hours—8 A.M. to 5 P.M., Monday through Friday. They like having evenings and weekends free and knowing exactly when they will work. But other people thrive on different hours. Maybe you're a night person who enjoys working evenings. Or maybe you prefer working on a Saturday and taking a day off in the middle of the week so that you can hit the beach when it's not crowded. Retail managers often work nights and weekends but have time off during the week to do their own thing.

Subjects to Study

Math, English, psychology, business courses, communication skills, computer skills

Discover More

Visit a shop in your neighborhood and ask the manager if you can help out after school one or two days a week. You might help stock shelves or clean up. Watch the manager at work and ask about the best and worst parts of the job.

Related Jobs

Financial managers, food service managers, lodging managers, medical and health services managers

Education & Training
Work experience

Earnings
$$$$

Job Outlook
Little change

Securities, Commodities & Financial Services Sales Agents

On the Job

Securities and commodities sales agents buy and sell stocks, bonds, and other financial products for clients who want to invest in the stock market. They explain terms and the advantages and disadvantages of different investments. Financial service sales agents usually work for banks. They contact potential customers to sell their bank's services, which might include retirement planning and other investment services.

Subjects to Study

Math, English, communication skills, computer skills, speech, accounting, economics, psychology, government, business courses

Education & Training
Bachelor's degree

Discover More

Find the stock market listings in the business section of your newspaper. Ask a parent or teacher to explain them to you. Listen to the stock market report on news programs or look up some stocks on the Internet.

Earnings
$$$$$

Related Jobs

Insurance sales agents, real estate brokers and sales agents, financial analysts and personal financial advisors

Job Outlook
Average increase

Travel Agents

On the Job

Travel agents make hotel, airline, car-rental, and cruise reservations for people and businesses. They plan group tours and conferences. They tell clients what papers they need to travel in foreign countries. They must be up-to-date on cultural and political issues, restaurants, and tourist attractions.

SOMETHING EXTRA

While the majority of travel agents plan getaways to the Bahamas or family cruises, some specialize in more unusual destinations. Whether it's planning a climb up Mount Kilimanjaro or tracking gorillas through the Bwindi Impenetrable Forest, there are agents out there who can plan that exotic trip for you. Though it probably wouldn't be cheap, it would certainly be memorable.

Subjects to Study

Communication skills, computer skills, geography, English, foreign languages, history, math, business courses

Discover More

What foreign country are you curious about? Read about that country and find it on a map. Then find an Internet site where you can learn more about life in that country. Finally, make a list of all the places you would like to visit in your life.

Related Jobs

Reservation and transportation ticket agents and travel clerks

Education & Training
Voc/tech training

Earnings
$$$

Job Outlook
Declining

Office & Administrative Support Occupations

Bill & Account Collectors

On the Job

Bill and account collectors keep track of accounts that are overdue and try to collect payment on them. Some are employed by collection agencies; others work directly for companies such as stores, hospitals, or banks. They use computers and special software to keep track of clients, and they spend a lot of time on the phone. Because money can be a sensitive matter, collectors must have good people skills while still being persistent.

Subjects to Study

Math, English, computer skills, business courses, accounting, psychology, foreign languages

Discover More

Spend half a day in the collection office of your local hospital. Talk to the collectors and ask about their most interesting cases. Many have wild stories about people going to great lengths to escape paying their bills.

Related Jobs

Credit authorizers, checkers, and clerks; loan officers; interviewers

Education & Training
Short-term OJT

Earnings
$$$

Job Outlook
Above-average increase

Billing & Posting Clerks & Machine Operators

On the Job

Billing and posting clerks keep records of customers' charges and payments. They calculate the total amount due from a customer and prepare a detailed bill showing any new charges and payments. Billing machine operators print out bills and invoices, which are then sent to customers.

SOMETHING EXTRA

You probably know what the word cramming means when it comes to studying for tests. But cramming also refers to unexplained charges—usually on your phone bill and often initiated by scam artists offering free contests or services. These unscrupulous individuals charge you for services you didn't even want or get, and it often just shows up as "Miscellaneous charges" on the bill. Sneaky.

Subjects to Study

Math, computer skills, office skills, English, accounting, bookkeeping, business courses

Discover More

Ask your parents to show you some of the bills they receive. What information is included on each bill? Ask what the terms "transaction date" and "closing date" mean. See if there are any additional charges that your parents can't explain.

Related Jobs

Payroll and timekeeping clerks; bookkeeping, accounting, and auditing clerks; tellers; order clerks

Education & Training
Moderate-term OJT

Earnings
$$$

Job Outlook
Little change

Bookkeeping, Accounting & Auditing Clerks

On the Job

Bookkeeping and accounting clerks keep records of all the money their company spends and receives. They prepare reports, post bank deposits, and pay bills. Auditing clerks check the financial records of other employees in an organization and correct any errors they find. These clerks must be careful in their work in order to ensure the accuracy of financial records. They also must be comfortable using computers.

Subjects to Study

Math, office skills, computer skills, English, business courses, accounting

Discover More

Keep your own financial records. Use a notebook to record any money you receive from allowance, gifts, or chores. Then record how you spend your money. Keep your receipts and banking records in a file.

Related Jobs

Bill and account collectors; billing and posting clerks and machine operators; brokerage clerks; credit authorizers, checkers, and clerks; payroll and timekeeping clerks; procurement clerks; tellers

Education & Training
Moderate-term OJT

Earnings
$$$

Job Outlook
Little change

Gaming Cage Workers

On the Job

Gaming cage workers, also called cage cashiers, work in casinos and other gaming companies. The "cage" they work in is the central depository for money, chips, and paperwork. They do credit checks on people who want to open a casino credit account and sell gambling chips, tokens, and tickets. They use cash registers, adding machines, and computers to add up transactions. They must follow strict rules and regulations when handling money.

SOMETHING EXTRA

Many people think of casinos as exotic, glamorous places. Some are, but many are not! Workers in gaming places must stand on their feet for long hours; deal with angry and upset customers—some of whom have had too much to drink—and breathe the smoke from other people's cigarettes. Turnover is high in this profession.

Subjects to Study

Math, business courses, English, foreign languages

Discover More

To learn about careers in the gaming industry, check out the Web site for the American Gaming Association: www.americangaming.org.

Related Jobs

Credit authorizers, checkers, and clerks; gaming service occupations; sales worker supervisors; cashiers; retail salespersons; tellers

Education & Training
Short-term OJT

Earnings
$$

Job Outlook
Average increase

Payroll & Timekeeping Clerks

On the Job

Payroll and timekeeping clerks make sure that workers get their paychecks on time and that the checks are for the right amount. Payroll clerks figure a worker's pay by adding up the hours worked and subtracting taxes, insurance, and other deductions. Timekeeping clerks collect timecards from employees and check them for errors. Many of these clerks perform other additional clerical tasks, such as file management and data entry.

Subjects to Study

Math, office skills, computer skills, English, accounting

Discover More

Ask your parents to show you their paycheck stubs. Notice the difference between the "gross" and "net" earnings. Find out what costs (such as insurance, taxes, and savings plans) are taken out of the paycheck. These are called "deductions."

Related Jobs

Bill and account collectors; billing and posting clerks and machine operators; bookkeeping, accounting, and auditing clerks; gaming cage workers; procurement clerks; tellers

Education & Training
Moderate-term OJT

Earnings
$$$$

Job Outlook
Average increase

Procurement Clerks

On the Job

Procurement clerks order the supplies and materials companies need to stay in business. They keep track of orders, making sure they arrive on schedule at the right price and meet the company's needs. These clerks perform inventory checks, keep spreadsheets, and place orders when stocks are short. They work in companies of all sizes and all kinds.

SOMETHING EXTRA

Procurement clerks used to be vital employees of most businesses. Today, however, with advances in technology, many clerks are being replaced by automated systems. Orders can be placed automatically as supplies get low. For example, many stores use cash registers that keep track of stock and place reorders whenever supplies go below a set level. Of course, some companies will always need a real human being to order inventory. But there are fewer today than yesterday.

Subjects to Study

Math, office skills, computer skills, English, foreign languages

Discover More

Try keeping track of inventory in your kitchen at home. Make a simple spreadsheet on graph paper or on the computer, noting how much of each item your family has on hand. When you notice something is getting low, write it down on a list hanging on the refrigerator so that it gets bought on the next grocery trip.

Related Jobs

Purchasing managers, buyers, and purchasing agents; order clerks; file clerks; secretaries and administrative assistants; receptionists and information clerks

Education & Training
Short-term OJT

Earnings
$$$$

Job Outlook
Declining

Tellers

Many people these days like to use their bank's automated teller machines (ATMs) to take out cash, make loan payments, and deposit money. ATMs are convenient because you can use them 24 hours a day, seven days a week. In fact, they are so convenient that some banks have started charging individuals to see an actual person to make a withdrawal rather than use the machine!

On the Job

Tellers work for banks, credit unions, and pension funds. They cash checks, make deposits and withdrawals, and accept loan payments. They use computers to keep records. Tellers begin work before the bank opens by counting the cash in their drawers and end the workday by accurately balancing their cash drawers with the day's receipts. They must be friendly with customers, even when customers are rude to them.

Subjects to Study

Math, English, communication skills, computer skills, foreign languages, accounting

Education & Training
Short-term OJT

Discover More

Open a savings or checking account at your local bank or credit union. Ask the teller to explain how to make deposits and withdrawals and how to use the ATM. Watch what the teller does as he or she helps you.

Earnings
$$

Related Jobs

Bill and account collectors; billing and posting clerks and machine operators; bookkeeping, accounting, and auditing clerks; gaming cage workers; brokerage clerks; credit authorizers, checkers, and clerks

Job Outlook
Little change

Brokerage Clerks

On the Job

Brokerage clerks record the sale and purchase of stocks, bonds, and other investments. They may contact customers, take orders, and inform clients of changes in their accounts. Most workers assist stock brokers, for whom they take calls from clients, write up order tickets, and process paperwork. Technology is changing their jobs today, as many now use special computer programs to process transactions.

SOMETHING EXTRA

Think you have what it takes to be a brokerage clerk? During bull markets (when stocks are generally rising), you will take orders, tell your customers how much money they've made, and hear lots of happy feedback. During bear markets (when stocks are falling), however, you might be the one who must tell a client that he or she has lost money. At these times, brokerage clerks need the people skills of a funeral director!

Subjects to Study

Math, business courses, office skills, computer skills, English, foreign languages, accounting

Discover More

You can learn more about the investment industry by checking out these Web sites on the Internet:

The Young Investor   www.younginvestor.com

Kids' Money   www.kidsmoney.org

EduStock   http://library.thinkquest.org/3088/

Related Jobs

Bill and account collectors; billing and posting clerks and machine operators; bookkeeping, accounting, and auditing clerks; order clerks; tellers

Education & Training
Moderate-term OJT

Earnings
$$$$

Job Outlook
Little change

Credit Authorizers, Checkers & Clerks

On the Job

Credit clerks collect and confirm information that people give when they apply for credit. Sometimes they investigate further by verifying employment or financial information. Credit checkers research credit records and decide whether customers or businesses have enough good credit to pay for what they want to buy. Credit authorizers approve charges on existing accounts.

Subjects to Study

English, communication skills, computer skills, math

Discover More

Ask your parents if they know what information is in their credit histories. What credit cards do they have? Ask them if they have a house or car loan. How much do they owe on their loans? Then, for fun, ask them if they will get you your own credit card (provided you don't have one already).

Education & Training
Short-term OJT

Earnings
$$$

Job Outlook
Declining

Related Jobs

Bill and account collectors, loan officers, insurance underwriters

Customer Service Representatives

On the Job

Customer service representatives work directly with customers, answering questions, taking orders, and solving problems. Many work for utilities, such as electric or gas companies or cable TV companies. They may handle billing mistakes, arrange for customers to have services switched on or off, and listen to lots of complaints. These workers spend a lot of time on the phone, and the work can often be repetitious and stressful.

Subjects to Study

English, foreign languages, psychology, office skills, computer skills

Discover More

The next time you have a problem with a product or service, pay special attention to how the customer service representative handles it. He or she must stay calm under pressure, be polite and helpful, and work quickly and efficiently. That's provided you get around to talking to a real live human being, of course.

Related Jobs

Tellers; insurance sales agents; securities, commodities, and financial services sales agents; retail salespersons; computer support specialists; gaming services occupations

Education & Training
Moderate-term OJT

Earnings
$$$

Job Outlook
Above-average increase

File Clerks

You can learn a lot about a business by working as a file clerk. For example, a file clerk at a law firm sees how legal documents are prepared. Insurance company file clerks learn about different types of claim forms. Working as a file clerk in a company can help you decide whether you are interested in learning more about that kind of business.

On the Job

File clerks sort, store, retrieve, and update office records filed according to a company's system. They examine incoming information and mark it with a number or letter code. They store the information in a paper file or enter the information into a computer file. When someone in the company needs information from a file, the clerk retrieves it. Because most filing is done electronically nowadays, filing clerks must be as comfortable around computers as they are around cabinets.

Subjects to Study

English, office skills, math, computer skills

Discover More

Set up a filing system at home using a file cabinet, folders, or a simple cardboard box. Keep your report cards, medical records, information about sports and activities, and your financial records in it. Make sure everything is clearly labeled and easy to find.

Related Jobs

Receptionists and information clerks; stock clerks and order fillers

Education & Training
Short-term OJT

Earnings
$$

Job Outlook
Declining

Hotel, Motel & Resort Desk Clerks

On the Job

Hotel, motel, and resort desk clerks help guests check in and out of the inn, using computers to assign rooms. They answer questions about the local area and the establishment itself. They keep records of room assignments and collect payment from guests. In smaller motels, desk clerks may also act as bookkeepers and switchboard operators.

> ### SOMETHING EXTRA
>
> So just what is the difference between a hotel and motel (besides a letter)? In general hotels tend to be nicer or offer more services than motels. But perhaps the most agreed-upon distinction is that at a hotel, the rooms have to be accessed from inside corridors, whereas at a motel the rooms are accessible from the outside. So then what does that make a hostel?

Subjects to Study

Math, English, geography, psychology, communication skills, speech, computer skills, foreign languages

Discover More

If you were a desk clerk at a hotel or motel in your town, what places would you suggest that guests visit? Which restaurants would you recommend? Make a visitor's guide for your community.

Related Jobs

Counter and rental clerks, customer service representatives, receptionists and information clerks, retail salespersons

Education & Training
Short-term OJT

Earnings
$

Job Outlook
Average increase

Human Resources Assistants, Except Payroll & Timekeeping

On the Job

Human resources assistants work with people who are applying for jobs in their company as well as with newly hired workers. They explain company rules, dress codes, pay policies, and benefits. They also maintain employee records and notify employees of job openings in the company. When conflicts arise at work, human resources workers help mediate them.

Subjects to Study

English, psychology, communication skills, office skills, computer skills, speech

Discover More

Get a job application from a business and look at the kind of information it asks for. Practice filling one out. If you can't get an application from a business, check the library for books with examples of job applications.

Related Jobs

Bookkeeping, accounting, and auditing clerks; communications equipment operators; customer service representatives; data entry and information processing workers; order clerks; receptionists and information clerks; secretaries and administrative assistants; stock clerks and order fillers

Education & Training
Short-term OJT

Earnings
$$$$

Job Outlook
Average increase

Interviewers

On the Job

Interviewers help people complete consumer surveys. New accounts clerks help people fill out bank account or charge card applications. They might work with people face to face, on the telephone, or by mail. Some interviewers get financial and medical information before admitting patients to a hospital. Others verify information or create new files. All must have good people skills.

SOMETHING EXTRA

Businesses use surveys to get all kinds of information. They might place a form in a magazine and ask readers to fill it out and send it in. Sometimes they hire people to call consumers and ask what brand of shampoo they buy or what TV shows they watch. Companies use this information to help them sell more of their products.

Subjects to Study

English, communication skills, math, psychology, sociology, foreign languages

Discover More

Take a survey to find out what books your friends are reading. Ask for each book's title and author. Has the person read other books by that author? What kinds of books are your friends reading? Do you notice any trends?

Related Jobs

Procurement clerks, customer service representatives, bill and account collectors

Education & Training
Short-term OJT to Moderate-term OJT

Earnings
$$$

Job Outlook
Little change

Library Assistants, Clerical

On the Job

Library assistants help librarians by working at the desk that lends and collects books, issuing library cards, and repairing books. They may provide special help to people who can't see well or to students looking for assignment materials. They file books when they are returned or left out and collect fines for overdue books. Many of them work part-time, making the job appealing to retirees, students, and others who need a flexible schedule.

Subjects to Study

English, math, computer skills, office skills

Discover More

Volunteer to clerk in your school library. Learn about the computer systems used in libraries to keep track of books, loans, overdue fines, and interlibrary loans. It's a long way from the old-fashioned card file.

Education & Training
Short-term OJT

Earnings
$$

Related Jobs

File clerks; human resources assistants, except payroll and timekeeping; order clerks; receptionists and information clerks; reservation and transportation ticket agents and travel clerks; librarians; library technicians

Job Outlook
Average increase

Order Clerks

On the Job

Order clerks receive and fill requests for machine parts, movie rentals, clothing, foods, and all kinds of other items. After completing the order, they send it to the proper department to be filled. They may fill orders from other employees inside a business, from salespeople, or from customers. Most work regular workday hours, but some must work nights and weekends.

SOMETHING EXTRA

Do you like to shop by phone, ordering things from catalogs? If so, you deal with order clerks. More than half of all order clerks work in wholesale or retail sales, and many of them work in catalog sales. These clerks receive orders by mail, e-mail, fax, or phone. They also handle customer questions and complaints. And they must remember the old rule, "The customer is always right!"

Subjects to Study

Math, English, foreign languages, computer skills, office skills

Discover More

Look through a catalog and read the directions for placing an order. Fill out the order form for the products you'd like to buy. Make sure you give all the information asked for on the form. Figure out what your order would cost, including tax and shipping charges.

Related Jobs

Stock clerks and order fillers; hotel, motel, and resort desk clerks

Education & Training
Short-term OJT

Earnings
$$$

Job Outlook
Declining

Receptionists & Information Clerks

Receptionists know who belongs where in an organization. Because of this, they are an important part of the security system at most companies. In larger companies, receptionists might give visitors identification cards or ask someone to escort a visitor to the proper office. They often are the first to meet visitors and the first to spot problems or suspicious characters.

On the Job

Receptionists greet customers on the phone and in person and refer them to the proper person or department. Making a good first impression is an important part of this job, as the receptionist is the first person most customers or clients meet. Some receptionists are responsible for coordinating incoming and outgoing mail as well. Information clerks file papers, make copies, do basic data entry, and may also be asked to answer phones in the front office.

Subjects to Study

English, communication skills, speech, computer skills, psychology, foreign languages, business courses, office skills

Discover More

Volunteer to be a greeter or an usher for a school play, a sports event, or a dance. Help people with their questions and concerns. Do you enjoy working with the public?

Related Jobs

Dispatchers, secretaries and administrative assistants, customer service representatives

Education & Training
Short-term OJT

Earnings
$$

Job Outlook
Above-average increase

Reservation & Transportation Ticket Agents & Travel Clerks

On the Job

Reservation and transportation ticket agents make and confirm travel and hotel reservations, answer questions about rates and routes, and sell tickets. Travel clerks plan trips and offer travel suggestions. They tell their clients about tourist attractions, quality hotels, and good restaurants. These clerks and agents might work for travel clubs, airlines, hotels, or other businesses.

SOMETHING EXTRA

Many people belong to automobile clubs. Members contact the club when they are planning a trip. They tell the travel clerk where they want to go and when. Then the travel clerk maps out the most convenient route for the trip. The map provides information about road construction, alternative routes, and scenic side trips. It also shows how many miles the trip will cover and how long it will take.

Subjects to Study

English, math, geography, communication skills, computer skills, history, psychology, foreign languages

Discover More

Look through travel magazines or the travel section of a newspaper. Pick somewhere you would like to visit and send for information about it or look up information about it on the Internet.

Related Jobs

Hotel, motel, and resort desk clerks; travel agents; flight attendants; counter and rental clerks; order clerks; customer service representatives; receptionists and information clerks

Education & Training
Short-term OJT

Earnings
$$$

Job Outlook
Little change

Cargo & Freight Agents

On the Job

Cargo and freight agents sort cargo according to where it is going, determine shipping rates and other costs, and then track the shipments. They take orders from customers and arrange for pickup of items for delivery to loading platforms. They also check on missing or damaged items. Cargo and freight agents work for air and railroad carriers, trucking services, and department stores. Some work in warehouses or outside on loading platforms may be required.

Subjects to Study

Math, English, foreign languages, business courses, bookkeeping, geography

Discover More

Call a freight service in your town and ask if you can spend a day shadowing a freight agent. Pay attention to the kinds of tasks he or she performs. Ask about the best and worst aspects of the job.

Related Jobs

Couriers and messengers; shipping, receiving, and traffic clerks; weighers, measurers, checkers, and samplers, recordkeeping; truck drivers and driver/sales workers; postal service workers

Education & Training
Moderate-term OJT

Earnings
$$$$

Job Outlook
Declining

Couriers & Messengers

On the Job

Messengers and couriers drive, walk, or ride bicycles to pick up and deliver letters and packages that must be delivered quickly—usually within a single city. Most work for courier services, although some work for law firms and many others are self-employed and provide their own vehicles. Some messengers are paid by how many deliveries they make and how far they travel.

Subjects to Study

English, foreign languages, driver's education, geography

Discover More

Start your own local courier service. Offer to deliver letters and packages at your school, church, or local hospital. You will pick up your packages at the main office and deliver them to other rooms in the building, or perhaps to other buildings.

Related Jobs

Postal service workers; truck drivers and driver/sales workers; shipping, receiving, and traffic clerks; cargo and freight agents

Education & Training
Short-term OJT

Earnings
$$

Job Outlook
Declining

Dispatchers

On the Job

Dispatchers receive emergency calls, find out where help is needed and how serious the situation is, and send police, firefighters, or ambulances to the scene. Dispatchers in transportation coordinate arrivals and departures of shipments to meet specific time schedules. All dispatchers keep records of the calls they receive and what they do about them. This kind of work can be stressful, especially in emergency situations.

Subjects to Study

English, computer skills, communication skills, psychology, foreign languages

Discover More

Learn how to contact emergency help in your community. Visit a fire or police station and ask for permission to watch a dispatcher work.

Related Jobs

Air traffic controllers, communications equipment operators, customer service representatives, reservation and transportation ticket agents and travel clerks

Education & Training
Moderate-term OJT

Earnings
$$$$

Job Outlook
Average increase

Meter Readers, Utilities

On the Job

Meter readers check electric, gas, water, or steam meters at businesses and houses and record how much has been used. They also inspect the meters for damage and contact repair workers if needed. They may turn off services if the customer does not pay the bill and turn on services for new customers. These workers drive or walk on their routes and spend a lot of time outdoors.

SOMETHING EXTRA

Technology is changing this field and causing a decline in the number of jobs. New automated meter-reading systems allow companies to monitor meters and bill customers from a central point. But it will be many years before these systems replace all meter readers, because most older homes and buildings still use the traditional meters. And the new systems cannot replace human beings in checking meters for damage or tampering.

Subjects to Study

Math, computer skills, business courses, bookkeeping

Discover More

Check the electric or gas meter on your own house or apartment. Track your family's use for one month. How much electricity or gas did you use? Now check the bill from the utility company. Do your figures match up? How much does the company charge per unit?

Related Jobs

Power plant operators, distributors, and dispatchers

Education & Training
Short-term OJT

Earnings
$$$

Job Outlook
Declining

Postal Service Workers

SOMETHING EXTRA

Stamps with errors in printing or design are often more valuable than the number printed on them—and gain value as they get older. Take for instance the world's most expensive stamp—a Swedish stamp that was printed in yellow-orange instead of green. It was discovered by a 14-year-old boy in 1885. It recently sold for more than two million dollars! Imagine finding that in your mailbox.

On the Job

The U.S. Postal Service delivers billions of pieces of mail each week. Postal workers sort mail for delivery, sell stamps, weigh packages, and help customers file claims for damaged packages. Mail sorters prepare incoming and outgoing mail for delivery. Mail carriers deliver the mail to homes and businesses on foot or by car in all kinds of weather. They also pick up mail from homes and businesses on their route.

Subjects to Study

English, physical education, driver's education, communication skills, computer skills

Education & Training
Short-term OJT

Discover More

Find out who delivers your mail and talk to your carrier about his or her job. Does your carrier walk or drive? What are the working hours? What does your carrier like or dislike about the job?

Earnings
$$$$

Related Jobs

Cashiers; counter and rental clerks; file clerks; shipping, receiving, and traffic clerks; couriers and messengers; truck drivers and driver/sales workers; inspectors, testers, sorters, samplers, and weighers; material moving occupations

Job Outlook
Declining

Production, Planning & Expediting Clerks

On the Job

These clerks coordinate the flow of information, work, and materials within or among offices. They set and review schedules, estimate costs, keep inventory of materials, inspect and assemble materials, and order replacements when supplies are low. Most work in manufacturing companies and in wholesale trade or grocery stores.

SOMETHING EXTRA

Have you heard the terms personnel supply services or temp agencies? They supply workers on a temporary basis to companies that don't want or need those workers full-time. Many production, planning, and expediting clerks are actually employed by temp agencies rather than the companies in which they do their work. This means less job security, of course, and often no benefits. But it's a good way to check out a job without making a long-term commitment.

Subjects to Study

Math, computer skills, business courses, bookkeeping, English

Discover More

Visit your local grocery and ask if you can spend a day with the people who do this job. You might help take inventory, order new supplies, answer phones, or check on overdue shipments. Don't forget to ask lots of questions.

Related Jobs

Cargo and freight agents; shipping, receiving, and traffic clerks; stock clerks and order fillers; weighers, measurers, checkers, and samplers, recordkeeping

Education & Training
Short-term OJT

Earnings
$$$$

Job Outlook
Little change

Shipping, Receiving & Traffic Clerks

Technology has changed the way warehouses operate. Many warehouse workers use handheld computer scanners, which help them check in goods more quickly. Some warehouses even have conveyer belts run by computers and robots that are able to move materials faster than people can move them. Gone are the days of the pencil and clipboard.

On the Job

Traffic clerks keep records of all freight coming in and leaving a company and make sure the company is charged correctly. Shipping clerks keep records on all outgoing shipments. They fill orders from the stockroom and direct workers who load products onto trucks. Receiving clerks check materials coming into the warehouse, make sure they are in good condition, and send them to the right departments.

Subjects to Study

Math, computer skills, business courses, bookkeeping

Discover More

Make a list of basic items you use every day, such as toothpaste, tissues, soap, and shampoo. Or make a list of the supplies you use at school. Check your personal inventory. What items do you need to restock?

Related Jobs

Stock clerks and order fillers; production, planning, and expediting clerks; cargo and freight agents; postal service workers

Education & Training
Short-term OJT

Earnings
$$

Job Outlook
Little change

Stock Clerks & Order Fillers

On the Job

Stock clerks receive, unpack, and check materials into the stockroom. They keep records of items entering and leaving the stockroom and report damaged or spoiled products. Order fillers bring items to the sales floor and stock shelves. They also gather items for shipment in mail-order companies. Many stock clerks work for department or grocery stores. The work can be physically strenuous.

SOMETHING EXTRA

An inventory is made up of all the products a business has on hand. A business must know what products it has if it is going to be successful. Bar code systems are the most popular way to track inventory. Bar codes are the black stripes you see on items you buy. Stock clerks use hand-held scanners to read bar codes. This helps keep the inventory accurate. Check out the bar code on the back of this book.

Subjects to Study

English, math, computer skills, physical education, bookkeeping

Discover More

Visit a grocery, retail, or warehouse-style store. Are there any stock clerks working on the floor? If so, notice how they organize products on the shelves. Ask what they like about the job.

Related Jobs

Shipping, receiving, and traffic clerks; production, planning, and expediting clerks; cargo and freight agents; procurement clerks

Education & Training
Short-term OJT

Earnings
$$

Job Outlook
Declining

Weighers, Measurers, Checkers & Samplers, Recordkeeping

On the Job

Just as the job titles imply, these workers weigh, measure, and check materials, supplies, and equipment to keep records. Most of their duties are clerical. They make sure that the amounts, quality, and value of things the company is buying matches what was ordered and paid for. They use weight scales, counting tools, tally sheets, computers, and calculators in their work.

Subjects to Study

Math, computer skills, business courses, bookkeeping

Discover More

Go along on a grocery-shopping trip with your parents. Take a tally sheet and a calculator. Record the price listed on each item and check it against the amount the cashier rings up. Keep a running total on the calculator as you go and check that amount against the cashier's as well.

Related Jobs

Cargo and freight agents; production, planning, and expediting clerks; shipping, receiving, and traffic clerks; stock clerks and order fillers; procurement clerks

Education & Training
Short-term OJT

Earnings
$$

Job Outlook
Declining

Communications Equipment Operators

On the Job

Most communications equipment operators are telephone operators, helping customers find the phone numbers they need, place collect calls, or make overseas calls. These operators are employed by large telephone companies. Switchboard operators work in offices, hospitals, and hotels helping to route incoming and outgoing phone calls. Communications equipment operators work in offices, usually wearing portable headgear that frees their hands for typing. They may work nights and weekends.

SOMETHING EXTRA

Do you love to talk on the phone? Do you like helping people? Can you stay calm under stressful circumstances? If so, telephone operator may be the job for you. These workers spend their days (or nights) answering questions and talking with people from all over the world and in all kinds of situations. Most simply want help locating a phone number or dialing long distance, but telephone operators have talked depressed people out of suicide, helped calm accident victims until the police arrived, and even talked expectant dads through delivering babies!

Subjects to Study

English, public speaking, computer skills, foreign languages

Discover More

For more information about a career as a communications equipment operator, contact the Communications Workers of America, 2725 El Camino Ave., Sacramento, CA 95821; (916) 484-9421. Or check out their Web site: www.cwa-union.org.

Related Jobs

Dispatchers; hotel, motel, and resort desk clerks; customer service representatives; receptionists and information clerks; reservation and transportation ticket agents and travel clerks

Education & Training
Short-term OJT

Earnings
$$

Job Outlook
Declining

Computer Operators

On the Job

Computer operators supervise computer hardware systems and keep them working smoothly. They watch for and try to prevent computer problems. On a daily basis, they might check the computer's controls and load tapes, paper, and discs as needed. When there is a computer error, they must locate and solve the problem. Computer operators may be required to work evening, night, and weekend shifts.

Subjects to Study

Math, English, communication skills, computer science, computer skills

Discover More

How do blind people use computers? Visit your local library and ask whether it has any talking or Braille computers. (Braille is a special kind of raised writing that blind people "read" with their fingertips.) Sit in front of the computer, close your eyes, and try to use it.

Education & Training
Moderate-term OJT

Earnings
$$$$

Job Outlook
Declining

Related Jobs

Computer software engineers; computer programmers; computer support specialists and systems administrators; data entry and information processing workers; computer systems analysts; secretaries and administrative assistants

Data Entry & Information Processing Workers

On the Job

Information processing workers set up and type reports, letters, manuscripts, and mailing labels. They may have other office duties as well, such as filing, answering telephones, and sorting mail. Data entry workers fill out forms that appear on computer screens or enter lists of items or numbers. Sometimes they also proofread and edit documents. These workers are susceptible to wrist, neck, and back injuries from prolonged sitting and typing.

Subjects to Study

English, office skills, computer skills, spelling and grammar

Discover More

Before you begin a career in this field, you must type at least 50 words per minute accurately. One way to learn to type faster is by typing to music. Start with something moderately slow (like a love song), and then work up to faster and faster beats. The more you practice, the easier it becomes!

Related Jobs

Dispatchers, communications equipment operators, court reporters, medical records and health information technicians, secretaries and administrative assistants, computer operators

Education & Training
Moderate-term OJT

Earnings
$$

Job Outlook
Declining

Desktop Publishers

SOMETHING EXTRA

Publishing has changed drastically in the last three decades. In the past, printers used the hot type method to print materials. They used molten lead to create individual letters, paragraphs, and full pages of text. Making changes to a page was nearly impossible once the type was set. Today, the hot type method has gone the way of the dodo. Sitting at a PC in your own home, you can produce publications that far surpass the works of old, making changes easily and quickly, and never go near molten lead at all!

On the Job

Desktop publishers use computers to format text, photos, charts, and other graphic elements to produce newsletters, magazines, calendars, business cards, newspapers, books, and other publications.

Most work in firms that handle commercial printing and in newspaper plants, but many are self-employed. This is one of the 10 fastest-growing jobs in the U.S.

Subjects to Study

Computer skills, office skills, art, graphic design, photography, English, business courses

Education & Training

Voc/tech training

Earnings

$$$$

Job Outlook

Above-average increase

Discover More

Use a personal computer at home or school to design your own newsletter, or volunteer to work on your school newspaper or yearbook. Look through several magazines and newsletters—what catches your eye? What would you change? Can you think of a more attractive way to present the material?

Related Jobs

Artists and related workers; commercial and industrial designers; news analysts, reporters, and correspondents; prepress technicians and workers; public relations specialists; writers and editors

Office & Administrative Support Worker Supervisors & Managers

On the Job

These supervisors and managers make sure their employees work efficiently. If supplies are low or equipment needs to be repaired, they order new supplies or contract with a repair service. They train new employees, plan their work, and check their progress. They evaluate their employees' work habits, recommend pay raises and promotions, and sometimes must fire a worker. They can be found in nearly every sector of the economy.

> **SOMETHING EXTRA**
>
> Many supervisors and managers meet with people in other states or even other countries by attending satellite conferences. Offices in several locations are linked together using a satellite signal so that all of the people attending can see and hear one another. This way, workers all over the world can meet together without anyone having to leave home. (Though it might have been more fun to fly out to Tokyo for a meeting rather than sitting at your conference table in Wichita.)

Subjects to Study

English, communication skills, computer skills, business courses, math, speech, psychology

Discover More

Volunteer to manage a group project. Assign different parts of the project to different people and check their progress. You'll notice that everyone has his or her own way of doing things. What differences do you notice in the way each person works? How do they respond to your leadership?

Related Jobs

Bookkeeping, accounting, and auditing clerks; customer service representatives; data entry and information processing workers; office clerks, general; receptionists and information clerks; order clerks

Education & Training
Work experience

Earnings
$$$$

Job Outlook
Little change

Office Clerks, General

On the Job

General office clerks work in all kinds of businesses, from doctors' offices to banks, from big law firms to small companies. Because a business's needs change from day to day, a clerk's job duties do, too. These workers file, type, keep records, prepare mailings, and proofread documents for mistakes. Senior clerks may be responsible for supervising other workers.

Subjects to Study

English, word processing, computer skills, math, office skills, bookkeeping, accounting, business courses

Discover More

Can you type? Typing well is important in this and almost any other job. Many offices require clerks to type at least 60 words per minute. Take a typing class, practice, and become a good typist.

Related Jobs

Bookkeeping, accounting, and auditing clerks; communications equipment operators; customer service representatives; data entry and information processing workers; order clerks; receptionists and information clerks; secretaries and administrative assistants; stock clerks and order fillers; tellers

Education & Training
Short-term OJT

Earnings
$$

Job Outlook
Little change

Secretaries & Administrative Assistants

On the Job

Secretaries and administrative assistants help keep offices organized and running smoothly. They schedule appointments, maintain files, type correspondence, greet visitors, and answer telephone calls. They work with office equipment such as computers, fax machines, and copiers. They may supervise clerks and other office workers. Some, such as medical and legal secretaries, do highly specialized work.

SOMETHING EXTRA

In the past, people thought of secretaries as low-level gophers, young women who typed, answered phones, and made coffee. Today's reality is much different. A secretary now is a kind of junior executive, the keeper of the office schedules and key information. Men and women working as secretaries often have access to confidential information and the company credit card. Most businesspeople know that a company is only as good as its secretaries!

Subjects to Study

English, spelling and grammar, speech, computer skills, office skills, math

Discover More

Talk to the secretaries at your school about their training and job duties. Develop some office skills, such as typing, filing, and word processing.

Related Jobs

Bookkeeping, accounting, and auditing clerks; receptionists and information clerks; court reporters; human resources assistants, except payroll and timekeeping; computer operators; data entry and information processing workers; paralegals and legal assistants; medical assistants; medical records and health information technicians

Education & Training
Moderate-term OJT to Voc/tech training

Earnings
$$$$

Job Outlook
Little change

Farming, Fishing & Forestry Occupations

Agricultural Workers

On the Job

Agricultural workers plant, grade, and sort farm products. They work with food crops, animals, trees, and plants. They may work indoors or outdoors, in all kinds of working conditions. Many work long, irregular hours in plants and on farms. Some work as inspectors, ensuring that the nation's food supply is safe. More than 8 out of 10 agricultural workers are farmworkers and laborers. Farming is one of the most dangerous jobs in the U.S.

Subjects to Study

Physical education, shop courses, driver's education, biology, botany

Discover More

Plant a garden in your yard or at a community plot. Try your hand at growing some food items: Broccoli, peppers, and tomatoes are easy starters. Look for nonchemical ways to control bugs and other pests. When your crop is ready, make a salad and treat your family to dinner!

Related Jobs

Fishers and fishing vessel operators; forest, conservation, and logging workers; grounds maintenance workers; animal care and service workers; veterinary technologists; veterinarians

Education & Training
Short-term OJT to Work experience

Earnings
$

Job Outlook
Declining

Fishers & Fishing Vessel Operators

On the Job

Fishers and fishing vessel operators catch and trap fish and seafood for the country's restaurants and grocery stores. The boat's captain plans and oversees the fishing, hires crew members, and arranges for the day's catch to be sold. The first mate is the captain's assistant and is in charge when the captain is not on duty. The boatswain helps the captain oversee the deckhands, who carry out the sailing and fishing operations. These workers may spend weeks or even months at sea, away from family and friends. The work is hard and sometimes dangerous, and employment can be seasonal.

SOMETHING EXTRA

Moby Dick, Herman Melville's classic book, tells the story of a sea captain's obsessive battle with a particularly vindictive white whale. Ahab and his crew spend months chasing down the huge beast, and the final epic battle takes the captain's life. These days, whale-hunting is illegal for all but a few Native American groups. But sailors on fishing vessels still spend months at a time on the ocean, battling fatigue and the elements—though few of them, if any, have wooden legs.

Subjects to Study

Physical education, shop courses, navigation, math, first aid

Discover More

Take a boating-safety course to learn more about sailing. To find one near you, check out BoatSafe Kids at www.boatsafe.com/kids/index.htm, which has information on classes, online courses, books, activities, and other Web sites.

Related Jobs

Water transportation occupations

Education & Training
Moderate-term OJT

Earnings
$$

Job Outlook
Declining

Forest, Conservation & Logging Workers

On the Job

Forest and conservation workers help develop and protect forests by planting new trees, fighting the pests and diseases that attack trees, and helping to control soil erosion. Timber cutters and loggers cut down thousands of acres of forests each year for the timber that is used for wood and paper products. Forest, conservation, and logging workers work outdoors in all kinds of weather. Their work is demanding and dangerous.

Subjects to Study

Physical education, first aid, shop courses, botany, biology

Discover More

Learn to identify the different kinds of trees in your area. Study a tree identification book and then visit a forest or park. How many trees can you identify?

Related Jobs

Conservation scientists and foresters, grounds maintenance workers, material moving operators

Education & Training
Moderate-term OJT

Earnings
$$$

Job Outlook
Little change

Construction Trades & Related Workers

Boilermakers

SOMETHING EXTRA

While the term boilermaker used to refer only to workers who actually made boilers, today members of the boilermakers' union do a wide variety of jobs in construction, ship-building, and manufacturing. Some work on power plants and oil refineries. Others make heavy machinery, heaters, or even golf balls. Some produce cement, wallboard, and bricks, while others mine coal and other minerals. All of these workers call themselves boilermakers.

On the Job

Boilermakers build boilers, vats, and other large tanks used for storing liquids and gases. Boilers supply steam for electric engines and for heating and power systems in buildings, factories, and ships. Because most boilers last for 35 years or more, repairing and maintaining them is a big part of a boilermaker's job. These workers use dangerous equipment, lift heavy items, and may work on ladders or scaffolding.

Subjects to Study

Math, shop courses, blueprint reading, welding

Discover More

Most boilermakers belong to labor unions. Find out which labor unions are active in your community. Contact one and ask about what the union does and how people become members. Or visit the International Brotherhood of Boilermakers' Web site at www.boilermakers.org.

Education & Training
Long-term OJT

Earnings
$$$$

Job Outlook
Average increase

Related Jobs

Assemblers and fabricators; machinists; industrial machinery mechanics and maintenance workers; millwrights; pipelayers, plumbers, pipefitters, and steamfitters; sheet metal workers; tool and die makers; welding, soldering, and brazing workers

Brickmasons, Blockmasons & Stonemasons

On the Job

These workers lay sidewalks and patios, build fireplaces, and install ornamental exteriors on buildings. Brickmasons work with firebrick linings in furnaces and with bricks. Blockmasons work with concrete blocks. Stonemasons work with natural and artificial stones. They often build walls on churches, office buildings, and hotels. These workers are outdoors in all types of weather. They must be strong enough to move heavy materials. Many are self-employed.

Subjects to Study

Math, mechanical drawing, shop courses, art, physical education

Discover More

You can learn more about brick and stonework training programs by checking out the International Masonry Institute's Web site at www.imiweb.org. Or call the Institute at 1-800-562-7464.

Related Jobs

Carpet, floor, and tile installers and finishers; cement masons, concrete finishers, segmental pavers, and terrazzo workers; plasterers and stucco masons

Education & Training
Long-term OJT

Earnings
$$$$

Job Outlook
Average increase

Carpenters

On the Job

Carpenters do all kinds of construction work, including woodworking, concrete work, drywall work, and many other jobs. They replace doors, windows, and locks; repair wooden furniture; hang kitchen cabinets; and install machinery. They work with hand and power tools and read blueprints. Carpenters form the largest group of building trade workers. Most work in new construction or remodeling. Others are self-employed.

Subjects to Study

Shop courses, mechanical drawing, carpentry, math

Discover More

Try a simple carpentry project such as building a doghouse, a shelf, or a flower box. First, get a plan and gather the materials you need. Be sure you know how to use your tools safely before you begin.

Related Jobs

Brickmasons, blockmasons, and stonemasons; cement masons, concrete finishers, segmental pavers, and terrazzo workers; electricians; pipelayers, plumbers, pipefitters, and steamfitters; plasterers and stucco masons

Education & Training
Long-term OJT

Earnings
$$$$

Job Outlook
Average increase

Carpet, Floor & Tile Installers & Finishers

On the Job

Carpet installers put carpet in new or old buildings and houses. Floor layers install flooring foundation materials such as rubber and linoleum, which act as sound dampers. Tilesetters use grout to apply ceramic tiles to floors and walls. All of these installers work regular daytime hours, but some work evenings as well. These workers spend their days kneeling, bending, stretching, and lifting heavy rolls of carpet and other materials.

SOMETHING EXTRA

Some people enjoy working 9 to 5 in an office. But others prefer traveling from place to place, working with their hands, and interacting with people. Carpet layers travel to people's homes and to office buildings, pull out old carpets, and lay down new carpeting. It's hard physical work—carrying rolls of carpeting and stretching and nailing down a new carpet—but every day they are in a new place, working on a new job, and meeting new people.

Subjects to Study

Shop courses, physical education, math, art

Discover More

Carpet installers must measure rooms precisely. Using a tape measure and a calculator, measure a room in your house. Include nooks, bends, and closets. Take the total width of the room and multiply by the total length to get the square footage.

Education & Training
Moderate-term OJT to Long-term OJT

Related Jobs

Brickmasons, blockmasons, and stonemasons; carpenters; cement masons, concrete finishers, segmental pavers, and terrazzo workers; drywall installers, ceiling tile installers, and tapers; painters and paperhangers; roofers; sheet metal workers

Earnings
$$$$

Job Outlook
Average increase

Cement Masons, Concrete Finishers, Segmental Pavers & Terrazzo Workers

On the Job

Cement masons and concrete finishers use a mixture of cement, gravel, sand, and water to build home patios, huge dams, and miles of roads. They pour the concrete and smooth the finished surface. Segmental pavers lay out flat pieces of masonry to form paths, patios, playgrounds, and driveways. Terrazzo workers add marble chips to the surface of concrete to create decorative walls, sidewalks, and panels. These workers spend their days outdoors, bending, stooping, and kneeling. Most wear kneepads and water-repellent boots for protection.

Subjects to Study

Shop courses, blueprint reading, mechanical drawing, physical education, math

Discover More

Most arts and crafts stores offer decorative concrete molds for making your own stepping stones. These kits require you to mix and pour the concrete, make imprints, and design and place decorative tiles. Ask a parent if they can help you make one for a friend or family member.

Related Jobs

Brickmasons, blockmasons, and stonemasons; carpet, floor, and tile installers and finishers; drywall installers, ceiling tile installers, and tapers

Education & Training
Moderate-term OJT to Long-term OJT

Earnings
$$$$

Job Outlook
Average increase

Construction & Building Inspectors

On the Job

Construction and building inspectors make sure that the country's buildings, roads, sewers, dams, and bridges are safe. They may check electrical or plumbing systems, elevators, or the beams and girders on skyscrapers. They climb high ladders, crawl through underground tunnels, and squeeze into tight spaces to do their jobs.

SOMETHING EXTRA

In 1989, a magnitude-6.8 earthquake hit Armenia in Central Asia. Thousands of buildings collapsed, killing more than 25,000 people. A year later, San Francisco was hit with an even larger earthquake, yet only 62 people died. Why the difference? Buildings, roads, and bridges in California must meet strict building codes. Those codes and the inspectors who enforce them saved thousands of lives.

Subjects to Study

Math, geometry, algebra, drafting, shop courses, computer skills

Discover More

Inspectors often use photographs in their reports. Practice your photography skills by taking pictures of building details in your neighborhood. Do you see anything that might be unsafe?

Related Jobs

Carpenters; plumbers; electricians; architects, except landscape and naval; construction managers; engineers; cost estimators; drafters; engineering technicians; surveyors, cartographers, photogrammetrists, and surveying technicians

Education & Training
Work experience

Earnings
$$$$

Job Outlook
Above-average increase

Construction Equipment Operators

On the Job

Construction equipment operators drive and operate the huge machinery used in building construction, road building and repair, and demolition. They might operate cranes, tractors, scrapers, backhoes, pavers, cement mixers, tamping machines, or hoists. They work outdoors in every kind of weather at construction sites, shipping docks, airports, mines, and on the nation's highways. The pay for these jobs can be high, but the work may slow down in bad weather, reducing earnings. The work schedule can be erratic as well, often requiring late night and early morning shifts.

Subjects to Study

Electronics, shop courses, science, physical education

Discover More

To learn more about jobs operating these huge machines, check out the Web site of the International Union of Operating Engineers, which offers apprenticeships and training programs: www.iuoe.org.

Related Jobs

Truck drivers and driver/sales workers, material moving occupations

Education & Training
Moderate-term OJT

Earnings
$$$$

Job Outlook
Average increase

Construction Laborers

On the Job

Construction laborers do a wide range of physically demanding jobs. They build skyscrapers and houses, roads, and mine shafts. They remove waste materials and help tear down buildings. The work can be dangerous when they work at great heights, remove hazardous chemicals, or work underground. Some work at construction only during the warmer months.

SOMETHING EXTRA

Who built the great pyramids of Egypt? If you answer the pharaohs, you are sadly mistaken. Certainly, the pharaohs funded the building of the pyramids, but it was construction laborers who did the actual building. Using only the technology of ancient times, these workers cut huge stones from quarries, shaped them into building blocks, moved them from the quarries to the building sites, and then raised them hundreds of feet, layer upon layer. It's a spectacular building feat, even by modern standards.

Subjects to Study

Shop courses, physical education, driver's education

Discover More

Offer your services to your family or neighbors the next time they are planning a construction project. You might help build a porch or deck, pave a driveway, or haul materials to and from the worksite.

Related Jobs

Material moving occupations; forest, conservation, and logging workers; grounds maintenance workers

Education & Training
Moderate-term OJT

Earnings
$$$

Job Outlook
Little change

Drywall Installers, Ceiling Tile Installers & Tapers

On the Job

In most buildings, the walls and ceilings are made of drywall. Drywall and ceiling tile workers fasten drywall panels to a building's framework. Then they fill the joints between boards and prepare the wall for decorating. They may put metal or gypsum lath on walls, ceilings, and frameworks for support. These workers spend their days standing, reaching, and bending. They work on ladders and high scaffolding and wear masks so that they don't breathe in the dust from their work. Many are self-employed.

Subjects to Study

Shop courses, carpentry, physical education, math

Discover More

Visit a hardware store or lumberyard and look at the drywall pieces. Ask the sales workers how the boards are cut and what tools drywall workers use.

Related Jobs

Carpenters; carpet, floor, and tile installers and finishers; insulation workers; plasterers and stucco masons

Education & Training
Moderate-term OJT

Earnings
$$$$

Job Outlook
Little change

Electricians

On the Job

Electricians work with the systems that provide electricity to homes and businesses. They may install wiring, heating, and air-conditioning systems, or make repairs to such systems. They must follow government rules and building codes to ensure their own safety and the safety of the buildings they work on. Electricians may work nights and weekends and be on call 24 hours a day. Many are self-employed.

SOMETHING EXTRA

Benjamin Franklin contributed a great deal to our understanding of electricity, including naming the electrical charges (positive and negative) and helping to prove that lightning was a form of electricity. You may have seen drawings or cartoons of Franklin flying a kite in a lightening storm, trying to harness electricity. While it is true that he performed this experiment, Franklin himself was not in the conducting path, or else he probably would have been electrocuted.

Subjects to Study

Math, shop courses, electronics, mechanical drawing, science, blueprint reading

Discover More

Can you get power from a lemon? Try this experiment using a strip of copper, a strip of zinc, a small flashlight bulb, and a lemon. Insert the metal strips into the lemon, close together but not touching. Now put the end of the light bulb on the zinc and the end of the copper on the threads. The acid in the lemon should make the bulb light up.

Education & Training
Long-term OJT

Earnings
$$$$

Related Jobs

Heating, air-conditioning, and refrigeration mechanics and installers; line installers and repairers; electrical and electronics installers and repairers; electronic home entertainment equipment installers and repairers

Job Outlook
Average increase

Elevator Installers & Repairers

On the Job

Elevator installers and repairers assemble, install, repair, and replace elevators and escalators. They repair and update older equipment and install new equipment. They also test the equipment to make sure it works properly.

These workers must have a thorough knowledge of electricity and electronics. They may be on call 24 hours a day to help out in an emergency.

Subjects to Study

Math, shop courses, science courses, electronics, physics

Discover More

Learn about apprenticeship programs by visiting the Web site of the International Union of Elevator Constructors at www.iuec.org.

Related Jobs

Boilermakers, electricians, electrical and electronics installers and repairers, industrial machinery mechanics and maintenance workers, sheet metal workers, structural and reinforcing iron and metal workers

Education & Training
Long-term OJT

Earnings
$$$$$

Job Outlook
Average increase

Glaziers

On the Job

Glaziers cut, install, and remove all kinds of glass and plastics in doors, windows, showers, and baths. They often use glass that is precut and mounted in a frame. They may use cranes to lift large, heavy pieces into place. Once the glass is mounted, glaziers secure it with bolts, cement, metal clips, or wood molding. Glaziers work outdoors in all kinds of weather. They sometimes work on ladders and high scaffolding.

SOMETHING EXTRA

You've probably heard of or seen stained glass, but do you know how it's made? These days, only a small portion of glasswork in windows is actually "stained." Most stained glass today is actually clear glass that's been painted with silver oxide or pot-metal glass that's been colored in its molten state. The earliest colored glass we know about today is from 306 B.C., when builders in the Far East used it for windows in homes and public buildings.

Subjects to Study

Shop courses, math, blueprint reading, mechanical drawing

Discover More

Make your own "stained glass" creation by getting a window-hanger kit from your local craft store. These kits contain metal frames and small, colored beads. You simply fill the frame with beads and then put it in the oven to melt the beads so that they look like glass.

Related Jobs

Brickmasons, blockmasons, and stonemasons; carpenters; carpet, floor, and tile installers and finishers; cement masons, concrete finishers, segmental pavers, and terrazzo workers; painters and paperhangers; automotive body and related repairers

Education & Training
Long-term OJT

Earnings
$$$$

Job Outlook
Average increase

Hazardous Materials Removal Workers

Did you know that, until the 1970s, lead was a common ingredient in house paint? Then researchers began proving that lead is toxic to humans—especially children. For years, people scraping old paint from their walls and windowsills had been releasing lead-filled dust into their homes and slowly poisoning their kids. Lead poisoning can lead to learning disabilities and lower IQs in children.

On the Job

These workers identify, remove, package, transport, and dispose of materials that are dangerous to human beings. They might deal with asbestos, lead, or radioactive materials. They wear protective clothing, including coveralls, gloves, shoe covers, face shields, and respirators. They must follow strict safety guidelines, and the work may require climbing or crawling into tight spaces. They may be called on to work overtime to meet deadlines or handle emergencies.

Subjects to Study

Math, chemistry, biology, physical education

Discover More

Do you know what kinds of hazardous materials are present in your community? To find out, check out Environmental Defense's Scorecard at www.scorecard.org. Just type in your ZIP code and you'll get a complete list of what pollutants are being released into the environment near you and who is releasing them.

Related Jobs

Painters and paperhangers; insulation workers; sheet metal workers; power plant operators, distributors, and dispatchers; water and liquid waste treatment plant and system operators

Education & Training
Moderate-term OJT

Earnings
$$$$

Job Outlook
Rapid increase

Insulation Workers

On the Job

Builders put insulation in buildings to save energy by keeping the heat in during the winter and the heat out during the summer. Insulation workers cement, staple, wire, tape, or spray insulation between the inner and outer walls or under the roof of a building. They often use a hose or blowing machine to spray a liquid insulation that dries into place. These workers must wear protective suits, masks, and respirators. Many are self-employed.

SOMETHING EXTRA

Have you ever heard of asbestos? It's a material that was once widely used for insulation in homes and buildings across America. It is fire-resistant and very effective. Unfortunately, it also causes cancer in people exposed to it. Insulation workers who deal with asbestos must wear special protective clothing, gloves, and masks to prevent asbestos contamination.

Subjects to Study

Shop courses, blueprint reading, physical education

Discover More

Head to your local hardware store and check out the different kinds of insulation. Ask the sales worker about each kind. Ask your parents what kind of insulation your home has. If you live in an apartment building, ask the building manager.

Related Jobs

Carpenters; carpet, floor, and tile installers and finishers; drywall installers, ceiling tile installers, and tapers; roofers; sheet metal workers

Education & Training
Moderate-term OJT

Earnings
$$$$

Job Outlook
Little change

Painters & Paperhangers

On the Job

Painters and paperhangers make walls look clean and attractive by applying paint or wallpaper to them. They paint outside walls with special paints that protect the walls from weather damage. Painters mix paints to match colors, then brush and roll the paints onto surfaces. Sometimes they rag-roll, splatter, or sponge on a second coat of paint in a different color. Paperhangers apply sizing and wallpapers and add decorative borders. Many are self-employed and work outdoors or seasonally.

Subjects to Study

Shop courses, art, math, physical education

Education & Training
Moderate-term OJT

Earnings
$$$$

Job Outlook
Average increase

Discover More

Try your painting skills by refinishing an old piece of furniture. First, sand off the old finishing. Then clean the surface completely. Apply two or three even coats of a new color and then coat the surface with a clear finish.

Related Jobs

Carpenters; carpet, floor, and tile installers and finishers; drywall installers, ceiling tile installers, and tapers; painting and coating workers, except construction and maintenance; plasterers and stucco masons

Pipelayers, Plumbers, Pipefitters & Steamfitters

On the Job

Plumbers install and repair water, waste disposal, drainage, and gas pipe systems in homes and other buildings. They also install showers, sinks, toilets, and appliances. Pipelayers, pipefitters, and steamfitters install and repair the pipe systems used in manufacturing, creating electricity, and heating and cooling buildings. These workers may work nights and weekends, or be on call 24 hours a day. They must be strong enough to lift heavy pipes. Many are self-employed.

SOMETHING EXTRA

We may think of indoor plumbing as a modern convenience, or maybe we just take it for granted. But did you know that cultures as far back as 2600 B.C. had flush toilets attached to an elaborate sewage system? The Indus Valley Civilization had one in nearly every house, paving the way for Egyptian plumbing advances and the Roman aqueducts.

Subjects to Study

Shop courses, drafting, blueprint reading, physics, physical education, math

Discover More

Tour your home or school and look at the pipe work in the bathrooms and kitchen. Are the pipes lead, stainless steel, plastic, or copper? Are the joints taped or welded? Are there other kinds of piping in the building?

Related Jobs

Boilermakers; electricians; elevator installers and repairers; heating, air-conditioning, and refrigeration mechanics and installers; industrial machinery mechanics and maintenance workers; millwrights; sheet metal workers; stationary engineers and boiler operators

Education & Training
Moderate-term OJT to Long-term OJT

Earnings
$$$$

Job Outlook
Average increase

Plasterers & Stucco Masons

On the Job

Plasterers apply plaster to walls and ceilings to make them fire-resistant and more sound-proof. They also apply insulation to the outside of new or old buildings. They create smooth or textured finishes using trowels and combs. Skilled plasterers sometimes specialize in complicated decorative work. Stucco masons apply stucco finishes to exterior walls. Many plasterers and stucco masons are self-employed. Their work is physically demanding.

Subjects to Study

Mechanical drawing, shop courses, art, drafting, blueprint reading, physical education, math

Education & Training
Long-term OJT

Discover More

Make garden stones for your home or school. Mix plaster of paris and pour it into a flat, round mold. Place marbles, beads, and small shells in patterns in the wet plaster. Allow the plaster to dry and then remove the mold.

Earnings
$$$$

Related Jobs

Brickmasons, blockmasons, and stonemasons; cement masons, concrete finishers, segmental pavers, and terrazzo workers; drywall installers, ceiling tile installers, and tapers

Job Outlook
Little change

Roofers

On the Job

Roofers install roofs made of tar or asphalt and gravel, rubber, metal, and other materials. They may install or repair the tiles on private home roofs, or repair old roofs on other buildings. Some also waterproof concrete walls and floors. These workers do physically demanding work outdoors, including lifting, climbing, and stooping. They risk injury from slips, falls, and burns. The roofing industry has the highest accident rate of all construction work.

SOMETHING EXTRA

In the 1970s, James Taylor re-recorded a song called "Up on the Roof." In it, Taylor sang about escaping from the worries of the world and sitting on the rooftop, just relaxing. In reality, rooftops can be steep, slippery, scary places. They're not a good place for daydreaming, and roofing is not a good job for those who are careless or afraid of heights.

Subjects to Study

Shop courses, mechanical drawing, physical education, math

Discover More

Make a survey of roofing materials in your neighborhood. How many houses and buildings have asphalt-shingled roofs? Are there any buildings in your area with metal roofs or wooden shingles? How many are missing shingles?

Related Jobs

Carpenters; carpet, floor, and tile installers and finishers; cement masons, concrete finishers, segmental pavers, and terrazzo workers; drywall installers, ceiling tile installers, and tapers; plasterers and stucco masons; sheet metal workers

Education & Training
Moderate-term OJT

Earnings
$$$$

Job Outlook
Average increase

Sheet Metal Workers

You may already know that many insulation workers in the 1970s were exposed to asbestos—an insulation that causes cancer in humans. But did you know that sheet metal workers had high exposures, too? In a survey taken in the late 1980s, more than 31 percent of sheet metal workers in construction, shipyard, and refinery work showed signs of asbestos-related diseases.

On the Job

Sheet metal workers use large sheets of metal to make ductwork for air-conditioning and heating systems. They also make roofs, rain gutters, skylights, outdoor signs, and other products. They install and maintain these products as well. They usually work in shops or at the job site. They must be strong enough to lift heavy, bulky items. They wear safety glasses to protect their eyes, and they cannot wear jewelry or loose-fitting clothing around the machinery they use.

Subjects to Study

Algebra, geometry, mechanical drawing, shop courses, physical education

Discover More

To learn more about this job, write to the International Training Institute for the Sheet Metal and Air Conditioning Industry, 601 N. Fairfax St., Suite 240, Alexandria, VA 22314; or you can visit their Web site at www.sheetmetal-iti.org.

Education & Training
Moderate-term OJT

Earnings
$$$$

Related Jobs

Assemblers and fabricators; machinists; machine setters, operators, and tenders—metal and plastics; tool and die makers; glaziers; heating, air-conditioning, and refrigeration mechanics and installers

Job Outlook
Average increase

Structural & Reinforcing Iron & Metal Workers

On the Job

These workers build the steel frames used to strengthen bridges, high-rise buildings, highways, and other structures. They install metal stairways, window frames, decorative ironwork, and other metal products. Some erect metal storage tanks and other pre-made buildings. Structural and reinforcing metalworkers work outdoors in extremely high places, on scaffolding and beams. They must be strong enough to lift heavy pieces of metal.

SOMETHING EXTRA

It took 8,000 tons of steel, 93,167 high-strength bolts, and a 250-ton crane to build a 5,000-foot drawbridge. All that and just 15 people. That's right. A crew of 14 ironworkers and one crane operator built the bridge that connected the cities of Portland and South Portland, Maine. In only two months they laid almost 1,000 feet of girders—which just goes to show, experienced ironworkers can accomplish almost anything!

Subjects to Study

Shop courses, mechanical drawing, blueprint reading, physical education

Discover More

You can learn more about the physics of bridge building by making your own bridge. Stack four books in two piles that are the same height, four inches apart. Now use an index card as a bridge between the stacks. How many pennies can you put on the card before the "bridge" collapses? Now move the books closer and arch your bridge. Will it hold more pennies?

Related Jobs

Assemblers and fabricators; boilermakers; engineers; cement masons, concrete finishers, segmental pavers, and terrazzo workers; welding, soldering, and brazing workers

Education & Training
Long-term OJT

Earnings
$$$$

Job Outlook
Average increase

Installation, Maintenance & Repair Occupations

Computer, Automated Teller & Office Machine Repairers

On the Job

Computer repairers install and fix computers and equipment used with computers. Office machine repairers work on copiers, typewriters, cash registers, and mailing equipment. Some repairers work on both computers and office equipment. Automated teller repairers install and fix ATMs at banks and credit unions. These repairers work in many industries, and some are on call 24 hours a day to make emergency repairs.

Subjects to Study

Math, computer science, physics, shop courses, electronics

Education & Training
Voc/tech training

Earnings
$$$$

Job Outlook
Little change

Discover More

Do you know how to hook up a computer? Ask the teacher in your school's computer lab to show you how to connect a computer's cables to the printer or scanner. Ask whether the school uses a power-surge protector to prevent electrical overload.

Related Jobs

Broadcast and sound engineering technicians and radio operators, electronic home entertainment equipment installers and repairers, electrical and electronics installers and repairers, industrial machinery mechanics and maintenance workers, radio and telecommunications equipment installers and repairers

Electrical & Electronics Installers & Repairers

On the Job

These workers install and repair equipment in factories. About one-third of them work for the federal government, many for the Department of Defense. They install radar, missile controls, and communication systems on ships, on aircraft, on tanks, and in buildings. Other electronic equipment repairers work for telephone companies, at hospitals, and in repair shops.

SOMETHING EXTRA

Since the first bands of nomads started arguing over territory, armies have been coming up with new ways to throw weapons at their enemies. During the Middle Ages, warriors used catapults to launch stones, dead horses, and even manure into enemy camps. Gunpowder and the first guns brought that kind of warfare to an end. Today's warriors use computers to guide missiles to their targets—which is a lot cleaner than loading manure onto a catapult!

Subjects to Study

Math, physics, science courses, shop courses, electronics

Discover More

You can work on electronics projects in a science club or 4-H club. Ask your teacher whether one of these clubs meets at your school.

Related Jobs

Broadcast and sound technicians and radio operators; computer, automated teller, and office machine repairers; electronic home entertainment equipment installers and repairers; radio and telecommunications equipment installers and repairers; industrial machinery mechanics and maintenance workers

Education & Training
Voc/tech training

Earnings
$$$$

Job Outlook
Little change

Electronic Home Entertainment Equipment Installers & Repairers

On the Job

These workers install and repair radios, TV sets, stereos, cameras, video games, and other home electronic equipment. They run tests to find problems and adjust and replace parts. They sometimes use complicated equipment to help them detect problems. Most work in repair shops or in service departments at larger stores. They may make home visits to fix equipment. Some are self-employed.

Subjects to Study

Math, science courses, shop courses, electronics, physics

Discover More

Visit a home electronics repair shop in your area. Ask the technicians whether you can watch as they make repairs and run tests.

Related Jobs

Broadcast and sound engineering technicians and radio operators; computer, automated teller, and office machine repairers; electrical and electronics installers and repairers; radio and telecommunications equipment installers and repairers

Education & Training
Voc/tech training

Earnings
$$$

Job Outlook
Little change

Radio & Telecommunications Equipment Installers & Repairers

On the Job

These workers install, repair, and maintain complex telephone and radio equipment. Most work either in a phone company's central office or in the field at customers' homes or offices. Others work on equipment for cable TV companies, railroads, or airlines. Some work nights and weekends, and they may be on call to handle emergencies.

SOMETHING EXTRA

Communications equipment has changed a lot in the last 100 years. Before 1876, if you wanted to get in touch with people across town, you had to write a letter or go to their house. Today, you can connect with people in Mongolia or Zimbabwe instantly by phone or through the Internet. We have become a global village.

Subjects to Study

Math, science courses, shop courses, electronics, physics

Discover More

Take apart an old telephone and look at its insides. Can you follow the wires to their sources? Can you figure out what the different parts do? Now, can you put it back together?

Related Jobs

Broadcast and sound engineering technicians and radio operators; computer, automated teller, and office machine repairers; electronic home entertainment equipment installers and repairers; electrical and electronics installers and repairers; line installers and repairers; engineering technicians

Education & Training
Long-term OJT to Voc/tech training

Earnings
$$$$

Job Outlook
Declining

Aircraft & Avionics Equipment Mechanics & Service Technicians

On the Job

Aircraft and avionics mechanics and service technicians inspect airplanes for problems. They make repairs and test equipment to make sure it is working properly. Some work on several different types of planes, whereas others specialize in just one type. Some mechanics even specialize in one part of an aircraft, such as the engine or electrical system of a DC-10. Sometimes they work inside, but often they work outdoors.

Subjects to Study

Math, physics, chemistry, electronics, computer science, mechanical drawing

Discover More

To find out more about aircraft mechanics, write to the Flight Safety Foundation, 601 Madison Street, Suite 300, Alexandria, VA 22314. Or visit its Web site at www.flightsafety.org.

Related Jobs

Electricians, electrical and electronics installers and repairers, elevator installers and repairers

Education & Training
Voc/tech training

Earnings
$$$$

Job Outlook
Average increase

Automotive Body & Related Repairers

On the Job

Automotive body repairers fix cars and trucks damaged in accidents. They straighten bent bodies, hammer out dents, and replace parts that can't be fixed. Their supervisors usually decide which parts to fix, which ones to replace, and how long the job should take. In large shops, some repairers specialize in one type of repair, such as installing glass or repairing doors.

Subjects to Study

Shop courses, automotive body repair, science courses, math

Discover More

A model car has many of the same body parts as a real car. Buy a model car kit and build and paint the model. Can you customize the car so that it reflects your personality?

Related Jobs

Automotive service technicians and mechanics; diesel service technicians and mechanics; painting and coating workers, except construction and maintenance

Education & Training
Long-term OJT

Earnings
$$$$

Job Outlook
Average increase

Automotive Service Technicians & Mechanics

You've probably heard of the Indy 500. It's one of the biggest events of the year for racing pros. But you might not know just how expensive it is to race a car at Indy. For example, pit-crew mechanics change all four tires on a racecar seven times during each race. And each set of tires costs $1,200. That's $8,400 in tires alone. What do you suppose it costs to replace an engine?

On the Job

Automotive mechanics and service technicians repair and service cars, trucks, and vans that have gas engines.

Mechanics must be quick and accurate when they are diagnosing mechanical problems. During routine service work, mechanics inspect, adjust, and replace vehicle parts. They usually follow a checklist to make sure they examine parts that might cause a future breakdown. Some mechanics are self-employed. This job is becoming more and more technically demanding as automobiles become more complex.

Subjects to Study

Math, shop courses, automotive mechanics, electronics, computer skills

Education & Training
Voc/tech training

Earnings
$$$$

Job Outlook
Average increase

Discover More

Do you know someone who works on cars? Ask that person whether you can help or just watch while he or she works on a car. You can learn a lot by watching and listening as a mechanic works. You might even be able to help by handing him or her tools.

Related Jobs

Automotive body and related repairers, diesel service technicians and mechanics, small engine mechanics

Diesel Service Technicians & Mechanics

On the Job

Diesel mechanics and service technicians repair and maintain diesel engines in heavy trucks, buses, and other equipment such as tractors, bulldozers, and cranes. They spend a lot of time doing preventive maintenance to make sure that the equipment operates safely, to prevent wear and tear, and to reduce expensive breakdowns. Most work in repair shops, but some work outdoors to repair equipment at construction sites.

SOMETHING EXTRA

Diesel engines are heavier and last longer than gas engines. They're also more efficient because a diesel engine compresses its fuel—so it uses less to do more. This means that more fuel is available to power the engine. Large trucks, buses, trains, and even some cars have diesel engines these days. But although diesel fuel is more efficient, it might be harder to find at your local gas station.

Subjects to Study

Math, shop courses, automotive repair, electronics, computer skills

Discover More

Do you know the differences between gas engines and diesel engines? You can find out by reading about engines and how they work. Check out some science books from the library and learn about both kinds of engines, or research it at www.howstuffworks.com/diesel1.htm.

Related Jobs

Aircraft and avionics equipment mechanics and service technicians, automotive service technicians and mechanics, heavy vehicle and mobile equipment service technicians and mechanics, small engine mechanics

Education & Training
Voc/tech training

Earnings
$$$$

Job Outlook
Average increase

Heavy Vehicle & Mobile Equipment Service Technicians & Mechanics

When a big piece of machinery breaks down at a logging site or a mine, the workers can't simply pack it up and bring it into the repair shop. That's where a field service mechanic comes in. These workers drive specially equipped trucks to the work site to make the repair. They might be on the job for a week or two before they're off to the next site. Many mechanics enjoy the independence of working outside the repair shop.

On the Job

These mechanics and technicians repair the machinery used in construction, logging, and mining. They fix and maintain motor graders, trenchers, backhoes, bulldozers, and cranes. They service and repair diesel engines and other machine parts. They may also repair the hydraulic lifts used to raise and lower scoops and shovels. These workers are outdoors in all kinds of weather.

Subjects to Study

Math, automobile mechanics, physics, chemistry, shop courses

Discover More

Visit a construction site and watch how the equipment moves and works. Talk to a construction worker about what happens when a machine breaks down.

Related Jobs

Aircraft and avionics equipment mechanics and service technicians, automotive service technicians and mechanics, diesel service technicians and mechanics, industrial machinery mechanics and maintenance workers, small engine mechanics

Education & Training
Long-term OJT to Voc/tech training

Earnings
$$$$

Job Outlook
Little change

Small Engine Mechanics

On the Job

Small engine mechanics do routine engine checkups and repair everything from chainsaws to yachts. The mechanic first talks with the owner to try to understand the problem. Then he or she runs tests to find the source of the problem. In some areas, mechanics may work much more during the summer than they do in the winter because use of motorcycles, boats, and lawnmowers is more frequent. Many of these workers are self-employed.

> ### SOMETHING EXTRA
>
> If you take a job in a restaurant, you wouldn't expect to bring your own pots and pans, would you? But mechanics often must provide their own hand tools for their work. Most beginning mechanics start out with the basics, such as wrenches, pliers, screwdrivers, and power drills. As they gain experience, they collect more tools. Experienced mechanics might have thousands of dollars invested in tools.

Subjects to Study

Math, small-engine repair, shop courses, science courses, electronics

Discover More

Ask your parents or neighbor whether you can help them prepare the lawnmower for spring use or winter storage. As you work, ask about the various parts of the motor.

Related Jobs

Automotive service technicians and mechanics, diesel service technicians and mechanics, heavy vehicle and mobile equipment service technicians and mechanics

Education & Training
Moderate-term OJT to Long-term OJT

Earnings
$$$

Job Outlook
Average increase

Coin, Vending & Amusement Machine Servicers & Repairers

On the Job

These servicers and repairers check coin-operated machines that offer entertainment, soft drinks, snacks, sandwiches, and other items for sale. They retrieve money, stock the machines, and make sure the machines are clean and working properly. Amusement machine servicers and repairers work on arcade games, slot machines and jukeboxes. These workers travel from place to place to make repairs. They may be outside in all kinds of weather.

Subjects to Study

Shop courses, electronics, machine repair, math

Education & Training
Moderate-term OJT

Discover More

The next time you see someone servicing a vending machine, stop and talk with him or her. Ask about the best and worst parts of the job. How much time does the repairer spend on the road?

Earnings
$$$

Related Jobs

Electrical and electronics installers and repairers; electronic home-entertainment equipment installers and repairers; heating, air-conditioning, and refrigeration mechanics and installers; home appliance repairers

Job Outlook
Little change

Heating, Air-Conditioning & Refrigeration Mechanics & Installers

On the Job

These mechanics help keep people comfortable by installing and repairing heating systems and air conditioners. They also help protect food and medicine that must be kept refrigerated. These workers maintain, diagnose, and correct problems within entire heating or cooling systems. They may work for large companies or be self-employed. They also must conform to strict guidelines to help protect the environment.

SOMETHING EXTRA

People working in this job can have a strong impact on the environment. CFCs are coolants used in older air-conditioning and refrigeration systems. Particles of CFCs are dangerous if they escape into the atmosphere. Escaped CFCs eat away at the ozone layer that protects plants, animals, and people from too much radiation. Nothing on Earth will survive if the ozone layer is completely destroyed. Responsible technicians are careful to protect the environment from CFCs.

Subjects to Study

Shop courses, math, electronics, mechanical drawing, physics, chemistry, blueprint reading, physical education

Discover More

Visit your local supermarket and ask to talk with someone who works in the frozen-food or dairy section. Ask how repairs are made to the cooling systems.

Related Jobs

Boilermakers; home appliance repairers; electricians; sheet metal workers; pipelayers, plumbers, pipefitters, and steamfitters

Education & Training
Long-term OJT

Earnings
$$$$

Job Outlook
Above-average increase

Home Appliance Repairers

On the Job

These workers repair ovens, washers, dryers, refrigerators, and other home appliances. They may also repair power tools such as saws and drills. First, they find the problem, then they replace or repair faulty parts. At the same time, they tighten, clean, and adjust other parts if needed. They must keep good records, prepare bills, and collect payments.

Subjects to Study

Shop courses, electronics, math, science courses

Discover More

Call a repair shop in your area and ask whether you can help in the shop for a day or two. Watch how the repairer works and help out by bringing tools, waiting on customers, or cleaning the shop.

Related Jobs

Electrical and electronics installers and repairers; electronic home entertainment equipment installers and repairers; small engine mechanics; coin, vending, and amusement machine servicers and repairers; heating, air-conditioning, and refrigeration mechanics and installers

Education & Training
Long-term OJT

Earnings
$$$$

Job Outlook
Little change

Industrial Machinery Mechanics & Maintenance Workers

On the Job

Industrial machinery workers install and maintain the machines in factories or plants to keep the work on schedule. Their work includes keeping machines and their parts oiled, tuned, and cleaned. When repairs are needed, the repairer must work quickly so that production is not delayed, which might cause the company to lose money. Sometimes this means making emergency repairs at night or on weekends.

SOMETHING EXTRA

Industrial machinery mechanics must be able to spot and fix little problems before they cause major break-downs. If a machine has a vibration that shouldn't be there, mechanics must find the source of the problem, such as a worn belt or loose bearing. The more repairs they make at early stages, the more money they save their employers down the road.

Subjects to Study

Mechanical drawing, math, blueprint reading, science courses, physics, electronics, physical education, computer skills

Discover More

Contact the office of a factory in your area and ask for a tour. Watch the machinery used in production. Ask your guide what would happen to the production schedule if an important piece of machinery broke down.

Related Jobs

Aircraft and avionics equipment mechanics and service technicians; automotive service technicians and mechanics; diesel service technicians and mechanics; elevator installers and repairers; heating, air-conditioning, and refrigeration mechanics and installers; heavy vehicle and mobile equipment service technicians and mechanics

Education & Training
Short-term OJT to Long-term OJT

Earnings
$$$$

Job Outlook
Little change

Line Installers & Repairers

How much information can pass through a cable as wide as a human hair? A lot! Fiber-optic cables are made of tiny strands of glass. These tiny strands carry electricity, phone service, and cable TV signals to homes and businesses. So powerful are these strands that one pair of optical fibers can carry more than 100,000 phone conversations at one time!

On the Job

Line installers and repairers lay the wires and cables that bring electricity, phone service, and cable TV signals into our homes. They clear lines of tree limbs, check them for damage, and make emergency repairs when needed. This job can be dangerous because installers and splicers work underground, high above ground, and with various chemicals and electricity. They work outside in all kinds of weather.

Subjects to Study

Math, physical education, shop courses, science courses, electronics

Discover More

Contact the human resources department of your local electric company, telephone company, or cable TV company. Ask about the kinds of jobs they have and what kind of training they require.

Education & Training
Long-term OJT

Related Jobs

Broadcast and sound engineering technicians and radio operators, electricians, radio and telecommunications equipment installers and repairers

Earnings
$$$$

Job Outlook
Little change

Maintenance and Repair Workers, General

On the Job

General maintenance and repair workers have skills in many different crafts. They repair and maintain machines, mechanical equipment, and buildings and work on plumbing, electrical, and air-conditioning and heating systems. They build partitions, make plaster or drywall repairs, and fix or paint roofs, windows, doors, floors, woodwork, and other parts of building structures. They also maintain and repair specialized equipment and machinery found in cafeterias, laundries, hospitals, stores, offices, and factories.

SOMETHING EXTRA

These days, just about everyone needs to know something about computers, including general maintenance workers. New buildings sometimes have computer-controlled systems, requiring workers to acquire basic computer skills. For example, new air-conditioning systems often can be controlled from a central computer terminal. General maintenance workers have yet another skill to add to their vast repertoire.

Subjects to Study

Mechanical drawing, electricity, woodworking, blueprint reading, science courses, math, computer skills

Discover More

Spend a day on the job with your school custodian. You'll find that they do much more than sweep the halls. They are responsible for making sure all the machinery in your school building works properly as well.

Related Jobs

Carpenters; pipelayers, plumbers, pipefitters, and steamfitters; electricians; heating, air-conditioning, and refrigeration mechanics and installers; electrical and electronics installers and repairers

Education & Training
Moderate-term OJT

Earnings
$$$$

Job Outlook
Average increase

Millwrights

On the Job

Millwrights install, repair, replace, and take apart the machinery and heavy equipment used in many industries. Most of them work in either manufacturing or construction. The wide range of facilities and the development of new technology require millwrights to keep their skills up-to-date—from blueprint reading and pouring concrete to diagnosing and solving mechanical problems. They work in a variety of settings from workshops to construction sites.

Subjects to Study

Science courses, math, mechanical drawing, computers, shop courses

Discover More

To see what kind of topics generally concern people who work as millwrights, go to the National Tooling and Machining Association Web site at www.ntma.org. Click on *Resource Center*, then *Discussion Forum*. This is where millwrights can share ideas and ask each other for advice to problems they have on the job.

Education & Training
Long-term OJT

Earnings
$$$$

Job Outlook
Little change

Related Jobs

Industrial machinery mechanics and maintenance workers; tool and die makers; structural and reinforcing iron and metal workers; assemblers and fabricators; heavy vehicle and mobile equipment service technicians and mechanics; welding, soldering, and brazing workers.

Precision Instrument & Equipment Repairers

On the Job

This job title covers a wide range of jobs. Precision instrument and equipment repairers fix watches and clocks, cameras, medical equipment, and even musical instruments. They use hand instruments and must have good eye-hand coordination and pay attention to details. Many are self-employed and work in small workshops. Musical instrument repairers often must travel to fix instruments onsite.

SOMETHING EXTRA

A piano tuner's tools include pliers, wire cutters, and various kinds of scrapers. Using a tuning fork, the tuner tightens or loosens the "A" string until it sounds like the tuning fork. Then he or she sets the pitch of each of the strings in relation to that "A" string. Tuning a piano this way requires a good ear, though many tuners now use electronic devices to match pitch.

Subjects to Study

Shop courses, carpentry, physical education, math

Discover More

Ask your band or orchestra teacher whether you can watch the next time he or she tunes the instruments or has a repairer come to work on them. Offer to help maintain the instruments.

Related Jobs

Computer, automated teller, and office machine repairers; coin, vending, and amusement machine servicers and repairers; dental laboratory technicians; ophthalmic laboratory technicians; industrial machinery mechanics and maintenance workers; jewelers and precious stone and metal workers; electronic home entertainment equipment installers and repairers

Education & Training
Moderate-term OJT to Associate degree

Earnings
$$$$

Job Outlook
Average increase

Production Occupations

Assemblers & Fabricators

Automation and robotics have eliminated many manufacturing jobs, but certain jobs are beyond a robot's abilities. A lot of precision assembly work is done in hard-to-reach places, such as inside gearboxes. Because robots are not flexible enough for such jobs, precision assemblers are less likely to be replaced by robots than other manufacturing workers.

On the Job

Assemblers and fabricators are experienced and trained workers who put together complicated products such as computers, appliances, and electronic equipment. Their work is detailed and must be done accurately. They follow directions from engineers and use several tools and precise measuring instruments. Some work in clean, well-lit rooms, while others work around grease, oil, and noise. They may have to lift and fit heavy objects.

Subjects to Study

Math, science, computer education, shop courses, electronics

Discover More

Get a kit from an electronics store and assemble a radio or another piece of electronic equipment. Alternatively, building model cars, planes, or rockets helps develop your assembly skills.

Related Jobs

Welding, soldering, and brazing workers; machine setters, operators, and tenders—metal and plastics; inspectors, testers, sorters, samplers, and weighers

Education & Training
Short-term OJT to Long-term OJT

Earnings
$$

Job Outlook
Little change

Food Processing Occupations

On the Job

Food processing workers work in grocery stores and production plants. They may work in a small market, in a large refrigerated room, or on an assembly line. Their work areas must be clean, but they are often cold and damp. Bakers produce cakes, breads, and other baked goods. Deli workers make salads and other side dishes. Butchers and meat, poultry, and fish cutters cut animal meat into small pieces to be sold to customers. These workers have the highest rate of work-related injuries and illnesses of any industry.

SOMETHING EXTRA

In the 1800s, a Swiss naturalist connected two facts. First, the brain contains phosphorus. Second, phosphorus is found in fish. Therefore, he decided that eating fish helps develop the brain. Actually, phosphorus is found in most foods, so eating fish before a test isn't a guarantee of getting an A. But it couldn't hurt!

Subjects to Study

Health, science courses, nutrition, family and consumer sciences, food preparation

Discover More

Learn about the different cuts of meat, fish, and poultry. Visit the meat department of a grocery store near you to see the different cuts. Talk to the butcher and ask about the job.

Related Jobs

Chefs, cooks, and food preparation workers

Education & Training
Short-term OJT to Long-term OJT

Earnings
$$

Job Outlook
Average increase

Computer-Control Programmers & Operators

On the Job

These workers use special computer-controlled machines to cut and shape products such as car parts, machine parts, and compressors. They follow blueprints from engineers. While they work they must constantly monitor readouts from the computer to make sure parts are being made properly. Because of the machinery they use, this can be a dangerous job.

Subjects to Study

Math, shop courses, blueprint reading, drafting, physics, mechanical drawing, computer skills, electronics

Education & Training
Moderate-term OJT to Long-term OJT

Earnings
$$$$

Job Outlook
Declining

Discover More

Visit a machining shop in your community and watch the programmers and operators at work. You may even be able to help by watching monitors and carrying parts.

Related Jobs

Machinists; tool and die makers; machine setters, operators, and tenders—metal and plastics; welding, soldering, and brazing workers; computer programmers

Machinists

On the Job

Machinists make metal parts using lathes, drill presses, and milling machines. They often make specialized parts or one-of-a-kind items for companies that produce everything from cars to computers. Most work in machine shops and wear safety glasses and earplugs. Because of the machinery they use and the coolants and lubricants for the machine, this can be a dangerous job.

SOMETHING EXTRA

What does a company do when it needs a special part for its one-of-a-kind machine? It hires a machinist to make the part. Machinists make everything from huge metal pincers to tiny metal bits—whatever the client needs. Some machinists even work making copies of antique tools and machinery for living museums and collectors. They use today's technologies to re-create yesterday's tools.

Subjects to Study

Math, shop courses, blueprint reading, drafting, physics, mechanical drawing, computer skills, electronics

Discover More

High school shops and vocational schools are some places you can find metalworking machines. Ask the instructor to show you how the machines work.

Related Jobs

Tool and die makers; machine setters, operators, and tenders—metal and plastics; computer-control programmers and operators; welding, soldering, and brazing workers

Education & Training
Long-term OJT

Earnings
$$$$

Job Outlook
Little change

Machine Setters, Operators & Tenders—Metal & Plastics

On the Job

These workers fall into two groups: those who set up machines for operation, and those who tend the machines while they work. They may work with drilling and boring machines, milling and planning machines, or lathe and turning machines.

They work according to blueprints and other instructions to turn out metal and plastic parts for everything from toasters to trucks.

Subjects to Study

Math, shop courses, blueprint reading, drafting, physics, computer skills, electronics

Education & Training
Moderate-term OJT

Earnings
$$$

Job Outlook
Declining

Discover More

Take apart an old appliance at home, such as a toaster or alarm clock. Separate the appliance into as many individual pieces as possible. Now look at the variety of shapes and sizes. Each individual part was made by machine setters and tenders.

Related Jobs

Machinists; tool and die makers; assemblers and fabricators; computer-control programmers and operators; welding, soldering, and brazing workers; inspectors, testers, sorters, samplers, and weighers

Tool & Die Makers

On the Job

Tool and die makers are highly skilled workers. Toolmakers create tools that cut, shape, and form metal and other materials. Die makers make dies, which are the forms used to shape metal in stamping and forging machines. Tool and die makers must know about machining operations, mathematics, and blueprint reading. They must follow safety rules and wear protective clothing on the job. They spend a good part of the day standing and must be able to lift heavy items.

SOMETHING EXTRA

Today's tool and die makers are on the cutting edge of technology. They use computer-aided design (CAD) programs to draw and test new parts and tools on the computer drawing board. Then they send the design to a computer-controlled machine that makes the actual part or tool. These workers also use special microscopes, micrometers, grinders, mills, and furnaces to do their jobs. The work requires a great deal of precision and attention to detail.

Subjects to Study

Math, shop courses, blueprint reading, drafting, mechanical drawing

Discover More

Using pen and paper, design a new tool to do something useful. Or think up a new use for an old tool. Can you convert an egg slicer to cut bagel chips? Can you think of a better tool for opening jars or cans?

Related Jobs

Machinists; computer-control programmers and operators; machine setters, operators, and tenders—metal and plastics; welding, soldering, and brazing workers

Education & Training
Long-term OJT

Earnings
$$$$

Job Outlook
Declining

Welding, Soldering & Brazing Workers

On the Job

These workers use the heat from a torch to permanently join metal parts. Because of its strength, welding is used to build ships, cars, aircraft, and even space shuttles. Welders may use a hand torch or a welding machine. They also use torches to cut and dismantle metal objects.

Welders must wear protective gear such as safety shoes and hoods with protective lenses to prevent burns and injuries. Some work outdoors on ladders or scaffolding.

Subjects to Study

Shop courses, blueprint reading, mechanical drawing, physics, chemistry

Discover More

To learn more about this occupation, write to the American Welding Society, 550 N.W. LeJeune Rd., Miami, FL 33126-5699; or check out its Web site at www.aws.org.

Related Jobs

Machinists; machine setters, operators, and tenders—metal and plastics; computer-control programmers and operators; tool and die makers; sheet metal workers; boilermakers; assemblers and fabricators

Education & Training
Moderate-term OJT to Long-term OJT

Earnings
$$$$

Job Outlook
Little change

Bookbinders & Bindery Workers

On the Job

Bookbinders and bindery workers use machines to "bind" the pages of books and magazines in a cover. These machines fold, cut, gather, glue, stitch, sew, trim, and wrap pages to form a book. Bindery work is physically hard. Workers stand, kneel, lift, and carry heavy items. Many work on assembly lines. Some work in hand binderies, and a few are self-employed.

SOMETHING EXTRA

Did you know that some rare old books are worth hundreds of thousands of dollars? So what does a library or museum do when one of these treasures starts to fall apart? They call in a bookbinder. These workers use special tools and chemicals to restore pages. Then they rebind the book by hand, using needle and thread. To help prevent books from deteriorating, many rare book libraries now require patrons to sit in environmentally controlled rooms and wear gloves.

Subjects to Study

Math, English, art, shop courses

Discover More

Bind your own book. First make an "end paper" by folding a sheet of heavy paper over your pages. Sew the pages into the end paper, using a heavy thread and needle. Paste each end paper to a heavy cardboard square. Now paste the squares onto a sheet of wallpaper. Cut the wallpaper to leave one inch of trim. Fold the trim over the cardboard squares and paste them down to make your book.

Related Jobs

Prepress technicians and workers; printing machine operators; machine setters, operators, and tenders—metal and plastics

Education & Training
Short-term OJT to Moderate-term OJT

Earnings
$$

Job Outlook
Declining

Prepress Technicians & Workers

On the Job

Prepress technicians and workers prepare materials for printing presses. They do typesetting, design page layouts, take photographs, and make printing plates. With personal computers, customers can now show workers how they want their printed material to look. Prepress workers have different titles depending on their jobs. Most work at video monitors, but some work with harmful chemicals.

Subjects to Study

English, electronics, computer skills, art, photography

Discover More

Learn how to use word processing and graphics programs on a computer. Industry standards include Microsoft Word, Corel WordPerfect, Adobe PageMaker and Photoshop, and Quark. Design your own greeting card, newsletter, or brochure.

Related Jobs

Artists and related workers, graphic designers, desktop publishers, data entry and information processing workers, printing machine operators

Education & Training
Long-term OJT

Earnings
$$$$

Job Outlook
Declining

Printing Machine Operators

On the Job

Printing machine operators prepare, run, and maintain the printing presses in a press-room. They check the paper and ink, make sure paper feeders are stocked, and monitor the presses as they are running. Computerized presses allow operators to make adjustments at a control panel by simply pressing buttons. These workers are on their feet most of the time. The work can be loud and physically demanding.

SOMETHING EXTRA

Before the Middle Ages, few people could read. That's because manuscripts had to be copied by hand. A group of workers called scribes were employed by monasteries to copy books. It was a time-consuming and expensive process. When a man named Gutenberg made the first printing press in 1456, he put a lot of scribes out of work. But he also made books available to the common man for the first time in history. Gutenberg's printing press is considered to be one of the most important inventions in human history.

Subjects to Study

Math, English, computer science, chemistry, electronics, physics

Discover More

Try printing your own greeting cards with a woodblock printing kit. These kits are available at craft and hobby stores.

Related Jobs

Machine setters, operators, and tenders—metal and plastics; bookbinders and bindery workers

Education & Training
Moderate-term OJT

Earnings
$$$

Job Outlook
Little change

Textile, Apparel & Furnishings Occupations

On the Job

Textile workers care for and operate the machines that make textile goods. These goods are then used in all kinds of products, from clothing to materials used in tires. Apparel workers make cloth, leather, and fur into clothing and other products. They may also repair torn or damaged items, or resew them to fit a customer better. Upholsterers are skilled craft workers who make new furniture or repair old furniture.

Subjects to Study

Family and consumer sciences, sewing, shop courses, woodworking, art, math, computer skills

Education & Training
Short-term OJT to Long-term OJT

Earnings
$$

Job Outlook
Declining

Discover More

Get a pattern for a simple sewing project from an arts and crafts store. Follow the pattern directions to make something you can wear.

Related Jobs

Assemblers and fabricators; medical, dental, and ophthalmic laboratory technicians; food-processing occupations; jewelers and precious stone and metal workers; woodworkers

Woodworkers

On the Job

Woodworkers make things from wood and work in many stages of the production process. They use machines that cut, shape, assemble, and finish wood to make doors, cabinets, paneling, and furniture. Precision woodworkers use hand tools to make rare or customized items. Most woodworkers handle heavy materials, stand for long periods, and risk exposure to dust and air pollutants. Some operate dangerous equipment.

SOMETHING EXTRA

If you think woodworkers make only furniture, think again! Woodworkers make a huge variety of items, from cabinets and rocking chairs to fishing decoys and jewelry. Some specialize in musical instruments such as guitars and banjoes. Others make knickknacks such as wooden flowers and jewelry boxes. Woodworkers even make machines from wood—imagine a wooden paper shredder. In fact, if you can dream it, a woodworker can probably make it.

Subjects to Study

Math, computer skills, shop courses, woodworking, blueprint reading

Discover More

Ask an adult to help you with a woodworking project, such as building a shelf or a wooden toy. You can get plans and materials for these projects at your local hardware store.

Related Jobs

Carpenters, sheet metal workers, structural and reinforcing iron and metal workers, computer-control programmers and operators, machinists, tool and die makers

Education & Training
Moderate-term OJT to Long-term OJT

Earnings
$$

Job Outlook
Declining

Power Plant Operators, Distributors & Dispatchers

On the Job

Power plant operators control the machinery that generates electricity. They start or stop generators as power requirements change. Power distributors and dispatchers make sure that users receive enough electricity by planning for times when more electricity is needed and handling emergencies. These workers often work nights, weekends, and holidays.

Subjects to Study

Math, physics, electronics, computer science, shop courses, English

Discover More

Talk to someone at the public relations department of your local electric company. Find out where your electricity is generated. Can your class take a field trip to tour the plant?

Related Jobs

Stationary engineers and boiler operators, water and liquid waste treatment plant and system operators

Education & Training
Long-term OJT

Earnings
$$$$$

Job Outlook
Declining

Stationary Engineers & Boiler Operators

On the Job

Stationary engineers and boiler operators operate and maintain equipment that provides air-conditioning, heat, and ventilation to large buildings. This equipment may supply electricity, steam, or other types of power. These workers may work weekends and holidays. They are exposed to heat, dust, dirt, and noise from the equipment. Hazards of the job include burns, electric shock, and injury from moving machinery parts.

SOMETHING EXTRA

One of the largest power plants in the U.S. is at the Hoover Dam on the Colorado River. With 17 generators, the plant provides low-cost power to cities and towns in Nevada, Arizona, and California—enough power to serve 1.3 million people. The dam was built during the Great Depression as part of a federal program that created jobs for the unemployed. Can you guess who was president at the time (wink, wink)?

Subjects to Study

Math, computer science, mechanical drawing, shop courses, chemistry

Discover More

Learn how to maintain and care for machines in your home such as the lawnmower and electric tools. Learn what tools to use, how to oil the machines, and how to keep them in good repair.

Related Jobs

Power plant operators, distributors, and dispatchers; water and liquid waste treatment plant and system operators; industrial machinery mechanics and maintenance workers; millwrights

Education & Training
Long-term OJT

Earnings
$$$$

Job Outlook
Little change

Water & Liquid Waste Treatment Plant & System Operators

On the Job

Water treatment plant operators make sure that the water you drink is safe. Wastewater plant operators remove harmful pollution from wastewater. They read meters and gauges and adjust controls. They take water samples, perform analyses, and test and adjust chemicals in the water, such as chlorine. They work both indoors and outdoors and may be exposed to dangerous gases. They may work day, evening, or night shifts; weekends; and holidays.

Subjects to Study

Math, chemistry, biology, shop courses, health, environmental sciences

Discover More

Call the water company in your community and ask whether your class can participate in a water-testing program. Many companies will send a representative to your school to teach a class on how to test the water at school and in your home for pollutants such as lead and harmful bacteria.

Related Jobs

Power plant operators, distributors, and dispatchers; stationary engineers and boiler operators

Education & Training
Long-term OJT

Earnings
$$$$

Job Outlook
Average increase

Inspectors, Testers, Sorters, Samplers & Weighers

On the Job

These workers examine and sort products before releasing them to consumers. They may test by looking, listening, feeling, tasting, weighing, or smelling. Products must meet certain quality standards. Inspectors may reject a product, send it back to be fixed, or fix the problem themselves. Inspectors work in all kinds of industries. Some move from place to place. Others sit on an assembly line all day.

SOMETHING EXTRA

How does a toy company ensure that each toy it produces is well made and safe for children? It hires inspectors to test them. A toy inspector might poke, pull, and drop a toy to see whether it breaks or measure it to see whether it might be a choking hazard for young children. Inspectors work in every industry that produces an item for sale. If a product is later found to have a defect, it has to be recalled and replaced at great cost to the company.

Subjects to Study

English, math, shop courses, blueprint reading, computer skills

Discover More

Learn how to contact a company if you are not satisfied with a product. Check the packaging of some products in your home for a consumer telephone number or an address. Call them and see what they will do for you.

Education & Training
Moderate-term OJT

Related Jobs

Construction and building inspectors, occupational health and safety specialists and technicians

Earnings
$$$

Job Outlook
Declining

Jewelers & Precious Stone & Metal Workers

On the Job

These workers use precious metals and stones such as gold and diamonds to make necklaces, rings, bracelets, and other jewelry. Some specialize in one area, such as buying, designing, cutting, repairing, selling, or appraising jewels. This work requires a high degree of skill and attention to detail. Jewelers use chemicals, sawing and drilling tools, and torches in their work. Some are self-employed.

Subjects to Study

Math, art, mechanical drawing, chemistry, computer skills, blueprint reading

Discover More

Take a jewelry-making class at school or your local craft store. Try designing and selling your own jewelry pieces.

Education & Training
Voc/tech training

Related Jobs

Precision instrument and equipment repairers; welding, soldering, and brazing workers; woodworkers; artists and related workers; fashion designers; retail salespersons; sales representatives, wholesale and manufacturing

Earnings
$$$

Job Outlook
Declining

Medical, Dental & Ophthalmic Laboratory Technicians

On the Job

Medical laboratory technicians construct artificial limbs, braces, and supports based on prescriptions from doctors. Dental laboratory technicians make the products dentists use to replace decayed teeth. Using dentists' directions and molds of patients' mouths, they make dentures (false teeth), crowns, and bridges. Ophthalmic laboratory technicians make the lenses for eyeglasses or for instruments like telescopes and binoculars.

SOMETHING EXTRA

What did people do before they had porcelain dentures? Did you know that when Elizabeth I was queen of England (1558–1603), she lost all her front teeth to decay? To make her face appear fuller, Elizabeth put pieces of cloth under her lips. Other members of the royal court had ornamental teeth made from silver or gold. The first "dentures" were made from bone or ivory, or just created from the teeth of dead or even living donors!

Subjects to Study

Science courses, art, shop courses, drafting, business math

Discover More

Visit an optical store at your local mall. Most have ophthalmic labs on site. Ask whether you can watch the technician work on a pair of glasses. Try on some frames while you're there.

Related Jobs

Dentists; opticians, dispensing; precision instrument and equipment repairers

Education & Training
Moderate-term OJT to Long-term OJT

Earnings
$$$

Job Outlook
Little change

Painting & Coating Workers, Except Construction & Maintenance

On the Job

Painting and coating machine operators cover everything from cars to candy with paints, plastics, varnishes, chocolates, or special solutions. The most common methods of applying paints and coatings are spraying and dipping. These workers must wear respirators over their noses and mouths to protect themselves from dangerous fumes. Most work in factories, but self-employed car painters may own their own shops.

Subjects to Study

Shop courses, art, chemistry

Discover More

An auto body repair shop is one place you can watch spray painting in action. Call a shop and ask if you can watch the painters. You will probably have to watch from a distance because of the fumes.

Related Jobs

Painters and paperhangers; woodworkers; machine setters, operators, and tenders—metal and plastics

Education & Training
Short-term OJT to Moderate-term OJT

Earnings
$$$

Job Outlook
Little change

Photographic Process Workers & Processing Machine Operators

On the Job

Photographic process workers and processors develop film, make picture prints and slides, and enlarge and retouch photographs. They also restore damaged and faded photographs. Most of these workers operate machines to complete their tasks. They are sometimes exposed to chemicals and must wear gloves and aprons for protection. Some work in large labs, while others work in one-hour mini-labs.

SOMETHING EXTRA

Did you ever hear the term photo finish? Sometimes in horse racing, two horses cross the finish line so close together that the human eye can't tell which was first. That's why there's a camera at the finish line of most racetracks. The camera records each finish. If there's a question about the finish, the photo is used to determine the winner. This leads to another phrase you've probably heard— "The camera doesn't lie!"

Subjects to Study

Math, art, computer science, photography

Discover More

Does your school have a darkroom? If so, find out who develops the photos for the school newspaper and yearbook. Ask if you can watch them do their work. Better yet, see if you can be become a photographer for the newspaper or yearbook and learn to do it yourself.

Related Jobs

Clinical laboratory technologists and technicians, computer operators, jewelers and precious stone and metal workers, prepress technicians and workers, printing machine operators, science technicians

Education & Training
Short-term OJT to Moderate-term OJT

Earnings
$$

Job Outlook
Declining

Semiconductor Processors

On the Job

Semiconductors, also known as microchips, are the tiny brains inside today's computers. Semiconductor processors are the workers who make these microchips. They work in sterile areas and wear special coveralls called "bunny suits" to keep any dust away from the chips. Operators use special equipment to imprint information on tiny silicon wafers. Technicians maintain the equipment and check the chips for flaws. Semiconductor plants operate around the clock, seven days a week, so shift work is common.

Subjects to Study

Math, physics, chemistry, computer science, electronics, shop courses

Education & Training
Associate degree

Discover More

To learn more about jobs as a semiconductor processor, write to the Maricopa Advanced Technology Education Center at 2323 West 14th St., Suite 540, Tempe, AZ, 85281, or visit their Web site at http://matec.org/ops/career.shtml.

Earnings
$$$

Related Jobs

Assemblers and fabricators, engineers, science technicians

Job Outlook
Declining

Transportation & Material Moving Occupations

On the Job

Aircraft pilots fly airplanes and helicopters, test aircraft, and sometimes fight forest fires. Pilots may work for large airlines, charter services, the government, or private businesses. They must plan flights, check the aircraft and weather conditions, and keep records of each flight. Flight engineers act as a third pilot on large aircraft, monitoring and operating many of the instruments and systems.

Subjects to Study

English, math, computer skills, electronics, geography, physics

Education & Training

Voc/tech training to Bachelor's degree

Discover More

If you are really interested in exploring this career, consider Aviation Career Education (ACE) Camp. This camp is designed for middle and high school students and lasts from one day to one week. For more information visit www.faa.gov/education_research/education/student_resources/ace_camps/.

Earnings

$$$$$

Related Jobs

Air traffic controllers

Job Outlook

Average increase

Air Traffic Controllers

On the Job

Air traffic controllers are responsible for the safe movement of airport traffic both in the air and on the ground. Using radar and visual observation, they direct landings, takeoffs, and ground movement of aircraft. They keep planes a safe distance apart during flights and inform pilots of current weather conditions. In emergencies they may search for missing aircraft. This can be a very stressful job.

SOMETHING EXTRA

Do you like computer games in which you have to keep track of a lot of small, moving objects? Imagine each of those objects as a real-life aircraft, carrying real human beings. Your job is to keep track of them, ensure they remain safely apart, and stay aware of changing conditions that affect them. Air traffic controllers must be able to track several aircraft, monitor weather and traffic, and stay calm under extreme stress.

Subjects to Study

English, math, computer skills, physics, shop and technology courses, foreign languages, electronics

Discover More

Call the U.S. Job Information Center in your area and ask for a copy of the *Air Traffic Controller Announcement,* which describes this job more fully. You can find the number in your Yellow Pages under U.S. Government, Office of Personnel Management. Or you can check the Web site for the National Air Traffic Controllers Association at www.natca.org.

Related Jobs

Aircraft pilots and flight engineers

Education & Training
Long-term OJT

Earnings
$$$$$

Job Outlook
Average increase

Bus Drivers

On the Job

Bus drivers transport people from place to place following a time schedule and a specific route. Some drive people long distances within a state or throughout the country. Others drive only locally. School bus drivers drive students to and from school. These workers deal with heavy traffic and many passengers, often in bad weather. Some work nights, weekends, and holidays; others travel overnight away from their homes. Many school bus drivers work part-time.

Subjects to Study

English, communication skills, math, driver's education, first aid

Discover More

Take a ride on a city bus and talk to the bus driver about this job. What tests does your state require? Is special training required? Watch what the driver does to communicate with passengers and care for the bus, but don't distract him or her too much.

Related Jobs

Taxi drivers and chauffeurs, truck drivers and driver/sales workers

Education & Training
Short-term OJT to Moderate-term OJT

Earnings
$$$

Job Outlook
Average increase

Taxi Drivers & Chauffeurs

On the Job

Taxi drivers and chauffeurs drive people in cars, limousines, and vans. Taxi drivers drive people to airports, hotels, or restaurants. Chauffeurs pamper their passengers by providing extras like newspapers, drinks, music, and television. These workers must lift heavy luggage and packages, drive in all kinds of weather and traffic, and sometimes put up with rude customers. Most taxi drivers and chauffeurs work nights and weekends.

Subjects to Study

English, math, physical education, driver's education

Discover More

Take a taxi ride and talk to the driver. Ask about the best and worst parts of the job. Has he or she ever driven anyone famous?

Related Jobs

Bus drivers, truck drivers and driver/sales workers

Education & Training
Short-term OJT

Earnings
$$

Job Outlook
Above-average increase

Truck Drivers & Driver/Sales Workers

On the Job

Truck drivers move and deliver goods between factories, terminals, warehouses, stores, and homes. They maintain their trucks, check for fuel and oil, make sure their brakes and lights work, and make minor repairs. They also load and unload the goods they transport. They drive in heavy traffic and bad weather. Some self-employed truckers may spend 240 days a year on the road.

Subjects to Study

Math, driver's education, physical education, accounting

Discover More

Call a truck driver training school in your area. Ask whether you can visit the school and see the rigs they drive. Maybe an instructor will take you for a ride.

Related Jobs

Bus drivers, taxi drivers and chauffeurs

Education & Training
Short-term OJT to Moderate-term OJT

Earnings
$$$

Job Outlook
Average increase

Rail Transportation Occupations

On the Job

This job includes railroad workers as well as subway and streetcar operators. Railroad engineers operate locomotives that transport passengers and cargo. Conductors are responsible for the cargo and passengers on trains. Brakemen remove cars and throw switches to allow trains to change tracks. Railroads operate around the clock, seven days a week. Employees work nights, weekends, and holidays. Some spend several nights a week away from home.

SOMETHING EXTRA

In the late 1800s, when the railroad was the best way to travel, wealthy people sometimes bought their own railroad cars. These cars were usually decorated with rich, expensive materials. Some even had luxury items such as sunken bathtubs, barber's chairs, and pipe organs. When they wanted to travel, these wealthy folks simply had their cars hitched to a train and traveled in style. Most employed their own maids, chefs, and waiters to serve them on the trip.

Subjects to Study

Math, geography, driver's education, physical education

Discover More

Visit a railroad station or ride a train or subway and watch the different workers. If they have free time, ask them about their jobs. What are the best and worst parts? Do they get to ride for free when they are off-duty?

Related Jobs

Bus drivers, truck drivers and driver/sales workers, water transportation occupations

Education & Training
Moderate-term OJT to Voc/tech training

Earnings
$$$$

Job Outlook
Declining

Water Transportation Occupations

On the Job

Workers in water transportation operate all kinds of boats on oceans, the Great Lakes, rivers, canals, and other waterways. Captains or masters are in charge of a vessel and the crew. Deck officers or mates help the captain. Seamen and deck hands do maintenance, steer, and load and unload cargo. Pilots guide ships through harbors and narrow waterways. These workers are outdoors in all kinds of weather. Many spend long periods away from home. Working on ships can be exciting, but also dangerous and lonely.

Subjects to Study

Math, physical education, swimming, first aid

Education & Training

Short-term OJT to Voc/tech training

Earnings

$$$$

Job Outlook

Little change

Discover More

Water transportation workers must be comfortable both on and in the water. Take swimming lessons at your local park or YMCA. Then sign up for a water-safety or first-aid course.

Related Jobs

Fishers and fishing vessel operators, job opportunities in the armed forces

Material Moving Occupations

On the Job

Material moving equipment operators and laborers load and unload trucks and ships using cranes, bulldozers, and forklifts. They move construction materials, logs, and coal around factories, warehouses, and construction sites. They sometimes set up, clean, and repair equipment. Most work outdoors in all kinds of weather. Others work inside warehouses or factories. The machinery may be noisy and dangerous.

SOMETHING EXTRA

Crane safety is a big concern today. That's because there are so many cranes operating on construction sites around the country, and they can be very dangerous. In 2004, a crane collapsed on a Toledo interstate highway, killing four people. That's why cranes are inspected regularly, and operators receive special safety training.

Subjects to Study

Shop classes, auto mechanics, driver's education, first aid

Discover More

Look for material moving machines in your community. What do they move? Are they used in any work except construction? How do the operators control the machines?

Related Jobs

Bus drivers; construction equipment operators; machine setters, operators, and tenders—metal and plastics; rail transportation occupations; truck drivers and driver/sales workers; construction laborers

Education & Training
Short-term OJT to Work experience

Earnings
$$

Job Outlook
Little change

Job Opportunities in the Armed Forces

Job Opportunities in the Armed Forces

On the Job

The U.S. armed forces is the country's largest employer. Maintaining a strong defense requires many activities, such as running hospitals, repairing helicopters, programming computers, and operating nuclear reactors. Military jobs range from clerical work to professional positions to construction work. People in the military must serve for a specified time and can be moved from one base to another. Many work nights, weekends, and holidays, and combat duty is always possible.

Subjects to Study

Math, English, business, science courses, shop courses, physical education

Discover More

Do you think you would enjoy military life? Talk to people who have served in the armed forces. Contact a recruiter to find out about a particular branch of the military. (Remember, though, that a recruiter's job is to get people to join.) Check the Military Careers Web site at www.militarycareers.com to learn about specific jobs within the military, as well as information about all five branches of the military (Army, Navy, Air Force, Marines, Coast Guard).

Education & Training
Moderate-term OJT to Work experience

Earnings
$$$

Job Outlook
Little change

Related Jobs

Nearly any civilian job

APPENDIX

More Job Information on the Web

The Internet is a great place to find out more about jobs that interest you. Here are some Web sites that will get you started.

General Career Exploration and Reference

Occupational Outlook Handbook Online
www.bls.gov/oco/

O*NET OnLine
http://online.onetcenter.org

America's Career InfoNet
www.acinet.org/acinet/

Career Guide to Industries
www.bls.gov/oco/cg/

Career Voyages
www.careervoyages.gov

CareerJournal.com
www.careerjournal.com

JobProfiles.org
www.jobprofiles.org

JIST Publishing
www.jist.com

Management and Business and Financial Operations Occupations

American Association of Advertising Agencies
www.aaaa.org

American Board of Funeral Service Education
www.abfse.org/index.html

American College of Health Care Administrators
www.achca.org

American Council for Construction Education
www.acce-hq.org

American Institute of Certified Public Accountants

www.aicpa.org

American Management Association

www.amanet.org

American Purchasing Society

www.american-purchasing.com

American Society of Farm Managers and Rural Appraisers

www.asfmra.org

Association for the Advancement of Cost Engineering

www.aacei.org

Association of Higher Education Facilities Officers

www.appa.org

Association of Management Consulting Firms

www.amcf.org

Association of University Programs in Health Administration

www.aupha.org

Community Associations Institute

www.caionline.org

Financial Management Association International

www.fma.org

Financial Planning Association

www.fpanet.org

Institute of Certified Professional Managers

http://cob.jmu.edu/icpm

Institute of Internal Auditors

www.theiia.org

Institute of Real Estate Management

www.irem.org

Insurance Information Institute

www.iii.org

Insurance Institute of America

www.aicpcu.org

International Claim Association

www.claim.org

International Council on Hotel, Restaurant, and Institutional Education

www.chrie.org

International Facility Management Association

www.ifma.org

Mortgage Bankers Association of America

www.mbaa.org

National Association of Elementary School Principals

www.naesp.org

National Association of Secondary School Principals

www.nassp.org

National Association of State
Budget Officers
www.nasbo.org

National Funeral Directors
Association
www.nfda.org

National Restaurant Association
Educational Foundation
www.nraef.org

Society for Human Resource
Management
www.shrm.org

Professional & Related Occupations

Aerospace Industries Association
www.aia-aerospace.org

Alliance of Cardiovascular
Professionals
www.acp-online.org

American Academy of Actuaries
www.actuary.org

American Academy of
Environmental Engineers
www.aaee.net

American Academy of Forensic
Sciences
www.aafs.org

American Academy of Physician
Assistants Information Center
www.aapa.org

American Anthropological
Association
www.aaanet.org

American Association for Laboratory
Animal Science
www.aalas.org

American Association for
Respiratory Care
www.aarc.org

American Association of Bioanalysts
www.aab.org

American Association of Colleges of
Pharmacy
www.aacp.org

American Association of Petroleum
Geologists
www.aapg.org

American Association of Pharma-
ceutical Scientists
www.aaps.org

American Bar Association
www.abanet.org

American Board of Opticianry
www.abo.org

American Chemical Society
www.acs.org

American Congress on Surveying and Mapping
www.acsm.net

American Correctional Association
www.aca.org

American Counseling Association
www.counseling.org

American Dental Association
www.ada.org

American Design Drafting Association
www.adda.org

American Dietetic Association
www.eatright.org

American Geological Institute
www.agiweb.org

American Health Information Management Association
www.ahima.org

American Historical Association
www.historians.org

American Institute of Architects
www.aia.org

American Institute of Biological Sciences
www.aibs.org

American Institute of Chemical Engineers
www.aiche.org

American Institute of Graphic Arts
www.aiga.org

American Institute of Physics
www.aip.org

American Library Association
www.ala.org

American Mathematical Society
www.ams.org

American Meteorological Society
www.ametsoc.org

American Nuclear Society
www.ans.org

American Occupational Therapy Association
www.aota.org

American Physical Society
www.aps.org

American Physical Therapy Association
www.apta.org

American Planning Association
www.planning.org

American Podiatric Medical Association
www.apma.org

American Political Science Association
www.apsanet.org

American Probation and Parole Association
www.appa-net.org

American Psychological Association
www.apa.org

American Society for Clinical Pathology
www.ascp.org

American Society for Engineering Education
www.asee.org

American Society for Microbiology
www.asm.org

American Society of Agricultural Engineers
www.asae.org

American Society of Agronomy
www.agronomy.org

American Society of Civil Engineers
www.asce.org

American Society of Health-System Pharmacists
www.ashp.org

American Society of Landscape Architects
www.asla.org

American Society of Mechanical Engineers
www.asme.org

American Society of Radiologic Technologists
www.asrt.org

American Society of Safety Engineers
www.asse.org

American Sociological Association
www.asanet.org

American Speech-Language-Hearing Association
www.asha.org

American Statistical Association
www.amstat.org

American Therapeutic Recreation Association
www.atra-tr.org

American Translators Association
www.atanet.org

American Veterinary Medical Association
www.avma.org

Archaeological Institute of America
www.archaeological.org

Association for Career and Technical Education
www.acteonline.org

Association for Computing Machinery

www.acm.org

Association of American Colleges and Universities

www.aacu.org

Association of American Geographers

www.aag.org

Association of American Medical Colleges

www.aamc.org

Association of Computer Support Specialists

www.acss.org

Association of Schools and Colleges of Optometry

www.opted.org

Association of Surgical Technologists

www.ast.org

Biomedical Engineering Society

www.bmes.org

Council of American Survey Research Organizations

www.casro.org

Council on Chiropractic Education

www.cce-usa.org

Division of Education, American Dental Hygienists' Association

www.adha.org

Institute for Operations Research and Management Science

www.informs.org

Institute of Electrical and Electronics Engineers

www.ieee.org

Institute of Electrical and Electronics Engineers Computer Society

www.computer.org

Institute of Industrial Engineers

www.iienet.org

Junior Engineering Technical Society (JETS-Guidance)

www.jets.org

Marketing Research Association

www.mra-net.org

Materials Research Society

www.mrs.org

Minerals, Metals, & Materials Society

www.tms.org

National Accrediting Agency for Clinical Laboratory Sciences

www.naacls.org

National Association for Business Economics

www.nabe.com

National Association for Practical Nurse Education and Service

www.napnes.org

National Association for the Education of Young Children
www.naeyc.org

National Association of Broadcasters
www.nab.org

National Association of Emergency Medical Technicians
www.naemt.org

National Association of Legal Assistants
www.nala.org

National Association of Schools of Art and Design
http://nasad.arts-accredit.org

National Association of Schools of Dance
http://nasd.arts-accredit.org

National Association of Schools of Music
http://nasm.arts-accredit.org

National Association of Schools of Public Affairs and Administration
www.naspaa.org

National Association of Schools of Theater
http://nast.arts-accredit.org

National Association of Social Workers
www.socialworkers.org

National Center for State Courts
www.ncsconline.org

National Clearinghouse for Professions in Special Education
www.special-ed-careers.org

National Court Reporters Association
www.ncraonline.org

National Federation of Paralegal Associations
www.paralegals.org

National High School Athletic Coaches Association
www.hscoaches.org

National League for Nursing
www.nln.org

National Organization for Human Service Education
http://nationalhumanservices.org

National Workforce Center for Emerging Technologies
www.nwcet.org

Pharmacy Technician Certification Board
www.ptcb.org

Professional Photographers of America
www.ppa.com

Public Relations Society of America
www.prsa.org

Society for American Archaeology
www.saa.org

Society for Mining, Metallurgy, and Exploration
www.smenet.org

Society for Technical Communication
www.stc.org

Society of American Archivists
www.archivists.org

Society of Broadcast Engineers
www.sbe.org

Society of Diagnostic Medical Sonography
www.sdms.org

Society of Nuclear Medicine
www.snm.org

Society of Petroleum Engineers
www.spe.org

U.S. Department of Education, Office of Vocational and Adult Education
www.ed.gov/about/offices/list/ovae

U.S. Department of Labor, Occupational Safety and Health Administration
www.osha.gov

Service Occupations

American Association of Medical Assistants
www.aama-ntl.org

American Association for Medical Transcription
www.aamt.org

American Council on Exercise
www.acefitness.org

American Dental Assistants Association
www.dentalassistant.org

American Gaming Association
www.americangaming.org

American Jail Association
www.corrections.com/aja/

Association of American Pesticide Control Officials
http://aapco.ceris.purdue.edu

Federal Bureau of Investigation (FBI)
www.fbi.gov

Humane Society of the United States
www.hsus.org

International Association of Firefighters
www.iaff.org

International Executive Housekeepers Association
www.ieha.org

National Animal Control Association
www.nacanet.org

National Association for Home Care
www.nahc.org

National Child Care Information Center
www.nccic.org

National Cosmetology Association
www.salonprofessionals.org

National Dog Groomers Association of America
www.nationaldoggroomers.com

National Restaurant Association
www.restaurant.org

Professional Lawn Care Association of America
www.plcaa.org

Tree Care Industry Association
www.TreeCareIndustry.org

Sales & Related Occupations

American Rental Association
www.ararental.org

American Society of Travel Agents
www.astanet.com

Independent Insurance Agents of America
www.iiaa.org

Insurance Vocational Education Student Training (InVEST)
www.investprogram.org

International Fabricare Institute
www.ifi.org

International Foodservice Distributors Association
www.ifdaonline.org

Manufacturers' Agents National Association
www.manaonline.org

Manufacturers' Representatives Educational Research Foundation
www.mrerf.org

National Association of Convenience Stores
www.nacsonline.com

National Association of Health Underwriters
www.nahu.org

National Association of Realtors
www.realtor.org

National Automobile Dealers Association
www.nada.org

National Retail Federation
www.nrf.com

Retail, Wholesale, and Department Store Union
www.rwdsu.info

Securities Industry Association
www.sia.com

Office & Administrative Support Occupations

Air Transport Association of America
www.airlines.org

American Institute of Professional Bookkeepers
www.aipb.org

Association of Computer Operations Management (AFCOM)
www.afcom.com

Association of Credit and Collection Professionals
www.acainternational.org

Association of Public Safety Communications Officials
www.apco911.org

Association for Suppliers of Printing, Publishing and Converting Technologies
www.npes.org/education/index.html

Communications Workers of America
www.cwa-union.org

Council on Library/Media Technicians
http://colt.ucr.edu

Educational Institute of the American Hotel and Lodging Association
www.ei-ahma.org

Graphic Arts Information Network
www.gain.net

International Association of
Administrative Professionals
www.iaap-hq.org

Legal Secretaries International
www.legalsecretaries.org

National Academies of Emergency
Dispatch
www.emergencydispatch.org

National Management Association
www.nma1.org

United States Postal Service
www.usps.com/about/

Farming, Fishing & Forestry Occupations

American Forest & Paper
Association
www.afandpa.org

Forest Resources Association
www.forestresources.org

Marine Technology Society
www.mtsociety.org

National FFA Organization
www.ffa.org

New England Small Farm Institute
www.smallfarm.org

Society of American Foresters
www.safnet.org

U.S. Forest Service
www.fs.fed.us

Construction Trades & Related Workers

American Society of Home
Inspectors
www.ashi.org

Associated General Contractors of
America
www.agc.org

Association of Construction
Inspectors
www.iami.org/aci/home.cfm

Brotherhood of Boilermakers
www.boilermakers.org

Floor Covering Installation
Contractors Association
www.fcica.com/index2.html

International Association of Bridge, Structural, Ornamental, and Reinforcing Iron Workers
www.ironworkers.org

International Association of Electrical Inspectors
www.iaei.org

International Masonry Institute
www.imiweb.org

International Union of Elevator Constructors
www.iuec.org

International Union of Operating Engineers
www.iuoe.org

International Union of Painters and Allied Trades
www.iupat.org

Laborers' International Union of North America
www.liuna.org

Laborers—AGC Education and Training Fund
www.laborerslearn.org

National Association of Home Builders
www.nahb.org

National Association of Plumbing-Heating-Cooling Contractors
www.phccweb.org

National Center for Construction Education and Research
www.nccer.org

National Concrete Masonry Association
www.ncma.org

National Electrical Contractors Association (NECA)
www.necanet.org

National Glass Association
www.glass.org

National Insulation Association
www.insulation.org

National Joint Apprenticeship Training Committee (NJATC)
www.njatc.org

National Roofing Contractors Association
www.nrca.net

Operative Plasterers' and Cement Masons' International Association of the United States and Canada
www.opcmia.org

Painting and Decorating Contractors of America
www.pdca.org

Sheet Metal Workers International Association
www.smwia.org

United Brotherhood of Carpenters and Joiners of America
www.carpenters.org

Installation, Maintenance & Repair Occupations

ACES International (Fiber Optics, Electronics, and Communications Professionals)
www.acesinternational.org

Air-Conditioning Contractors of America (ACCA)
www.acca.org

Association of Equipment Management Professionals
www.aemp.org

Automotive Service Association
www.asashop.org

Automotive Youth Educational Systems (AYES)
www.ayes.org

Computing Technology Industry Association
www.comptia.org

Custom Electronic Design and Installation Association
www.cedia.org

International Brotherhood of Electrical Workers
www.ibew.org

International Society of Certified Electronics Technicians
www.iscet.org

ISA—The Instrumentation, Systems, and Automation Society
www.isa.org

National Automatic Merchandising Association
www.vending.org

National Tooling and Machining Association
www.ntma.org

Professional Aviation Maintenance
Association
www.pama.org

SkillsUSA-VICA
www.skillsusa.org

Production Occupations

American Public Power Association
www.appanet.org

American Society for Quality
www.asq.org

American Textile Manufacturers
Institute
www.atmi.org

American Water Works Association
www.awwa.org

American Welding Society
www.aws.org

Graphic Communications Council
www.teched.vt.edu/gcc

Manufacturing Jewelers and
Suppliers of America
mjsa.polygon.net

National Association of Dental
Laboratories
www.nadl.org

Precision Machine Products
Association
www.pmpa.org

Precision Metalforming Association
Educational Foundation
www.pmaef.org

Semiconductor Industry Association
www.sia-online.org

Woodworker's Central
www.woodworking.org

Transportation & Material Moving Occupations

A Career Afloat
www.marad.dot.gov/acareerafloat

Air Line Pilots Association
www.alpa.org

American Public Transportation
Association
www.apta.com

American Trucking Association
www.trucking.org

Association of American Railroads
www.aar.org

Federal Aviation Administration
www.faa.gov

National Limousine Association
www.limo.org

National School Transportation Association
www.schooltrans.com

United Motorcoach Association
www.uma.org

Job Opportunities in the Armed Forces

Military Career Guide Online
www.todaysmilitary.com

INDEX OF JOB TITLES

O

P-Q

R

S

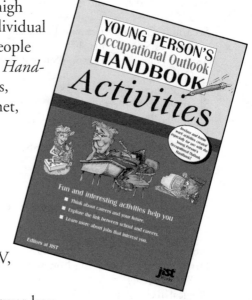